Cultivating a Child's Imagination
Through Gardening

Also by the Authors

Beyond the Bean Seed
Gardening Activities for Grades K-6
(Teacher Ideas Press, 1996)

Cultivating a Child's Imagination
Through Gardening

Nancy Allen Jurenka
and
Rosanne J. Blass

1996
TEACHER IDEAS PRESS
A Division of
Libraries Unlimited, Inc.
Englewood, Colorado

TEACHER IDEAS PRESS
A Division of
Libraries Unlimited, Inc.
P.O. Box 6633
Englewood, CO 80155-6633
1-800-237-6124

Production Editor: Stephen Haenel
Copy Editor: Lori Kranz
Proofreader: Suzanne Hawkins Burke
Design: Stephen Haenel and Michael Florman
Layout: Michael Florman

Library of Congress Cataloging-in-Publication Data

Jurenka, Nancy E. Allen, 1937-
    Cultivating a child's imagination through gardening / Nancy Allen Jurenka and Rosanne J. Blass.
        xiv, 144 p. 22x28 cm.
        Includes bibliographical references (p. 119) and index.
        ISBN 1-56308-452-X
        1. Children's gardens. 2. Gardening--Experiments. 3. Botany--Experiments. 4. Botany--Study and teaching--Activity programs.
5. Teaching--Aids and devices. I. Blass, Rosanne J., 1937-   .
II. Title.
SB457.J88 1996
372.3'57--dc20   96-32747
                                                              CIP

Contents

Acknowledgments

Librarians and their assistants in several libraries helped me locate the books for *Cultivating a Child's Imagination Through Gardening* and its companion book, *Beyond the Bean Seed*. For kind, patient, and tenacious helpfuness, I would like to thank children's and reference librarians at the Los Angeles Central, Tustin, California; Orange, California; Waynesboro, Pennsylvania; Yakima, Washington; King County, Washington; and the Corvalis and Albany, Oregon, public libraries.

I would especially like to acknowledge the service, expertise, helpfulness, and goodwill of the librarians and staff of the Ellensburg, Washington, Public Library: Carol Buchholtz, Paulette Fordan, Marianne Gordon, Verna Guatney, Sally Hammond, Rosemary Harrell, Celeste Kline, Carla Lewis, Jenny Mohora, Joan Neslund, Kerry Slaughter, Bonnie Turner, and Milton Wagy.

Karen Spence, Children's Services Coordinator for the Yakima Valley Regional Library provided instant answers to obscure questions.

Eve Pranis of the National Gardening Association deserves much praise for her national leadership and the work she is doing encouraging children to garden as well as her words of wisdom about gardening.

To Roy VanDenburgh, Yakima County Extension Agent for Horticulture, and Tom Hoffman, Kittitas County Extension Agent, thank you for effective leadership and coordination of the training programs for Master Gardeners that gave my life a new direction.

For stand-by-me friendship and waiting patiently, thank you Lee and Floyd Reeves. And for listening to tales of woe and triumph, thank you Sandy Thomas and Andrea Bowman. For word processing technical assistance and advice, Ginger Linnell and Luis and Becky Poblete have my gratitude. Patient and encouraging editors Stephen Haenel and Susan Zernial have shepherded this project through from beginning to end with grace and faith. Thank you.

Nancy Jurenka

Introduction

Purpose

Cultivating a Child's Imagination Through Gardening is a companion book to *Beyond the Bean Seed: Gardening Activities for Grades K-6*. Like its companion book, it uses children's literature, specifically, those works related to gardening, gardeners, designing gardens, multicultural literature, ecology, the environment, and the impact of plants on world economies and politics, to connect gardening in all its aspects to creativity, problem solving, imagination, and literacy. The purpose of this book is to provide garden-based experiences and literacy events designed to engage children in authentic relationships with the natural environment, adults, and peers.

The many activities developed in *Cultivating a Child's Imagination Through Gardening* include creative problem solving, brainstorming, flexible thinking, discovery learning, inventiveness, experiments with and exploration of the natural environment, as well as encouragement to dream, imagine, and fantasize. Art, color, design, folklore, literature, music, drama, dance, crafts, foods, and word play develop concepts that extend from the garden plot across cultures, continents, and centuries.

Like *Beyond the Bean Seed, Cultivating a Child's Imagination Through Gardening* is written for adults who garden with children: classroom teachers, arboretum and botanical garden educational directors, horticulturists, 4-H club leaders, librarians, parents, leaders of Cub Scouts, Boy Scouts, Brownie troops, Girl Scouts, and Campfire Girls, Bible School teachers, Master Gardeners, Cooperative Extension agents, gang prevention workers, social workers, nature and garden center teachers, homeschool parents, community and urban garden leaders and volunteers, retired people, and camp counselors. It is written to provide them with ideas for using children's books, language arts, and creative activities in a garden setting.

Topics not normally considered in the sphere of gardening—multicultural legends and folklore, fiction and biography, and social studies extensions such as geography, history, political science, economics, and marketing—were selected for this book. Response activities that provide opportunities to look beyond the ordinary were developed. Fiction, nonfiction, and poetry titles were chosen for their appropriateness to the activity and for their availability.

Topics, activities, and titles suggest and develop situations that engage children in reading, writing, listening, speaking, remembering, recalling, learning and relearning, representing, structuring, problem solving, and creating new solutions. Children are called upon to make connections between the immediate task and the wider world, between the natural environment and their own lives, between their experiences and their growing literacy development.

Cultivating a Child's Imagination Through Gardening is designed to contribute to the development of a community of learners that fosters a love for learning, literacy, and the environment through supportive interaction between children and adults.

Creativity

Definitions of Creativity

Amabile and Tighe (1993) state that while creativity should produce products that are appropriate and novel, creativity should also be heuristic in process. The process should be one that encourages open-ended investigation.

Madeleine L'Engle (1980) believes that all of us, particularly children, have the potential to be creative. Unfortunately, she observes, adults do things that stifle creativity. She states, "All children are artists and it is an indictment of our culture that so many of them lose their creativity, their unfettered imaginations, as they grow older. But they start off without self-consciousness as they paint their purple flowers, their anatomically impossible people, their thunderous, sulphurous skies" (p. 51).

Torrance (1979) believes that creativity is a skill that can be developed, not a talent possessed by only a chosen few.

May (1975) states that the creative process is a synthesizing of intellectual, volitional, and emotional functions. It is as if the creative person uses her knowledge purposefully and vehemently, even joyfully, to bring about a solution or product.

Encouraging Creativity

Although there are many explanations of creativity, Amabile and Tighe (1993) have an operational one that teachers will find applicable. They point out that creativity has three major components: 1) domain-relevant skills; 2) creativity-relevant skills; and 3) task motivation.

Having domain-relevant skills means that the person is knowledgeable about the topic or activity at hand; the person has the basic intelligence related to doing work within the subject area or domain. For the purposes of this book, it means that the children have a basic understanding and knowledge of botany and gardening skills that they will use as they create their gardens.

Creativity-relevant skills include these traits: able to produce many and varied ideas; can think independently; enjoy taking risks; able to deal with ambiguity; capable of perseverance; able to use categories to store information; and able to transcend previous mindsets. When teachers and youth leaders encourage the production of many alternative, out-of-the-ordinary solutions to gardening, design, literature, or other problems, they are encouraging these skills.

Task motivation refers to the degree to which the person is engaged in the creative process and whether or not motivation is intrinsic or extrinsic. One is not necessarily better than the other.

In addition, Amabile and Tighe (1993) point out that creativity and problem solving go hand in hand. They describe four stages of problem solving in which the components of creativity influence the success of the solution. Stage 1 is problem presentation; Stage 2 is preparation; Stage 3 is idea generation; and Stage 4 is validation.

In Stage 1 the problem is identified, formulated, and presented. At this stage, task motivation is needed. If a person could not care less at this point, the seeking of a solution is arrested. If the person is highly motivated, the imagining, feeling, and thinking processes are activated and focused upon finding a solution. Teachers and youth leaders need to be aware of the importance of the quality of motivation among their young gardeners. How much time needs to be spent front-loading an activity? How much insight and factual data will be needed before the children will comprehend the significance of the problem to be solved? The answers to these questions also relate to the seriousness of the problem or objective of the activity. For example, suppose your group has identified a particular area in your town that needs to be beautified. Before they commit themselves to this project, they need to know that they are in it for the long haul and that many questions will be begging for answers. Finding the answers will require perseverance. A measure of their motivation will need to be ascertained and maintained by the wise leader. On the other hand, perhaps all the group wishes to do is a simple craft project that requires a modicum of motivation to discover design solutions. The leader needs to be aware of the mix of extrinsic and intrinsic motivation required over time to successfully complete a creative project.

Stage 2, preparation, requires domain-relevant skills. Does the group have the basic knowledge and skills to take on the creative or problem-solving endeavor? If not, time will be needed to build the relevant skills and knowledge before the group can move forward toward success. This is the time to gather information and resources, read up on the topic, watch demonstrations, and listen to the experts necessary to complete the task at hand. Suppose you wanted to plant sedums and echeveria in odd-shaped containers. Does your group know what to look for? Do they know the cultivation requirements of these plants? Do they know how to plant them? Do they know what kind of soil is needed?

In Stage 3, idea generation, creativity-relevant skills are required as the children generate many diverse solutions to the problem.

In Stage 4, validation, the person asks: "Are these ideas appropriate?" "Is this a workable solution?" "Is this product useful?" "Will something good come from this answer?"

For a creative project to be successful, all these elements must be present. You need unusual and accurate problem-finding behaviors in Stage 1, a sufficient store of knowledge at Stage 2, unusual and workable solutions in Stage 3, and the idea finally selected in Stage 4 must maximize novelty and appropriateness. If one or more elements are missing, you will end up with no reasonable product or solution, or a product or solution that is technically correct but ho-hum, or a product or solution that is bizarre or unworkable.

While using these techniques demands more time of both adult and child, the payoff is worth it. By incorporating Amabile and Tighe's descriptions of and techniques for creative problem solving in their instructional repertoire, teachers and youth leaders involved in children's gardening programs will increase the heuristic problem-solving skills among the children with whom they work. The development and use of creativity are not "microwaveable"; they require time, perseverance, and hard work as well as artistry.

Applying Torrance's Questions to Garden Problem Solving

Paul Torrance, a well-known educator and writer in the field of creativity, suggests using heuristic questions to engage children in creative problem solving (1979, p. 16). It will be shown here how Torrance's types of heuristic questions might be applied to gardening. Torrance encourages us to:

- Engage children in the need to be aware of the necessity for problem identification and definition.

This may be done by confronting children with ambiguous or uncertain situations, as for example:

> Our garden will have no one to care for it during the next six weeks. What do you suggest?

> Our garden site is now the dirt bike trail for the neighborhood children. What shall we do?

- Have the children look at the problem from several perspectives: psychological, emotional, sociological, economical, political, etc.

Such a scheme may lead to the consideration of questions such as:

> What joy-filled activities will we have when we garden?

> What will be a real drag?

> How can we keep grasshoppers from demolishing our garden without doing harm to ourselves or the environment?

How can we repay or show our appreciation to the person who will rototill our garden plot?

How can we have dirt biking and gardening in the same area?

Is it reasonable to expect that we can grow orchids and poinsettias in this plot?

* Structure the problem simply.

What kinds of plants will grow in our garden? Why?

How do we know this?

* Reveal gaps in information and unsolved problems.

What don't we know about . . . ?

We need the approval of the Town Beautification Committee for our Pocket Park. How can we succeed in achieving this approval? Who do we need to convince?

* Call for going beyond what is known about something.

Suppose we wanted to design a garden that blind children, physically handicapped children, and children in wheelchairs could not just visit but work in all during the growing season. How shall we do this?

* Pose collision-type conflicts; juxtapose opposites.

We know that we have just the right type of soil, amount of rainfall and number of warm days to successfully grow yucca, ocotillo, cacti, and agave in our southwest desert area, but we really want to grow tomatoes and tulips. How can we do this?

* Pose future projections.

What would happen if we discovered a highly effective way to. . . ? How could we. . . ?

By following and applying Torrance's suggestions for questioning as well as Amabile and Tighe's ideas for the development of creative problem solving to gardening, your group will become more creative problem solvers, a talent your locality, state, and country need!

Imagination

What activities encourage imagination? One of the first things I did to prepare myself to write this passage was purchase colored drawing pencils in luscious colors. I know that when I want to get my imagination fired up, free drawing with many colors works every time.

Art Activities and Materials

Have on hand soft, colored pencils and lots of inexpensive paper. Janet Stevens, author and illustrator of *Tops and Bottoms,* made this suggestion at a reading conference. She observed that children are often frustrated by their first efforts at drawing and that they need many opportunities and materials to get their drawings done to their satisfaction.

Also, supply watercolors, tempera paint, brushes, water pots, newspaper, fingerpaint, shaving cream, sand, junk, throwaways, glue, play dough, clays, and papers of every type—crepe, tissue, cellophane, newsprint, coated, blueprint, manilla, construction.

Having these materials at the ready, you will be prepared for both planned and spontaneous art-related dreaming/imagining/planning activities as well as responses to a story or botanical or gardening event.

Art activities include imagining and drawing fantastic flowers, imaginary gardens, and spectacular insects, as well as keeping actual records of progress, say, the growth of the amaryllis, the life cycle of a butterfly being observed, or the garden spider found that morning in the children's garden.

Dance, Informal Dramatics, and Pantomime

Dancing is one of the best ways to get children in touch with their imagination. Torrance (1979) has a particularly successful idea: He suggests that multicolored pieces of nylon netting, 36 inches by 72 inches, be distributed among the children. These pieces of nylon netting act as aids to imagination when the children place them over their heads and imagine themselves to be a story character, scarecrow, rose, tree, pumpkin, or praying mantis come to life. Play programmatic music such as Tchaikovsky's *Nutcracker Suite,* Saint-Saens' *Carnival of the Animals,* or Schubert's *The Trout.* Encourage a few minutes of unstructured dancing. Combine dancing with children's literature by having the children respond by dancing to a garden-related story like Demi's *The Empty Pot.*

Along with the pieces of nylon netting, have on hand hats, ribbons, aprons, capes, period clothes, and secondhand clothing, as well as props such as magic wands, plastic swords, play telephones, and so on. You never know when the acting urge will hit, and if you are prepared with a well-stocked costume and prop box, success will result from impulse.

Children need many alternative forms of communication and self-expression. Dancing and informal dramatics increase imagination and communication.

Music

Listening to music and conjuring up the scenes suggested by the music generate imagination. Guided imagination activities could focus on having the children imagine gardening in a fantasy garden, walking inside gigantic colorful flowers, finding solutions to a problem, or responding to a gardening-related story. They could draw in a free-form manner while listening to music such as Scott Cossu's *Stained Glass Memories,* Pat Metheny's *Watercolors,* or movements from Prokofiev's *Romeo and Juliet* or Mussorgsky's *Night on Bald Mountain.*

Quiet Reflective Times

Quiet reflective times are essential to the generation, encouragement, and development of imagination and creativity.

Madeleine L'Engle, writing in *Walking on Water,* describes the duty of the artist to "slow down" and to "listen to the silence," a phrase inscribed on a poster given to her by the sisters at the Convent of the Transfiguration. Silence, she points out, is necessary for the creative person to receive inspiration and insight concerning the creative endeavor to which he or she has committed herself (1980, p. 12).

There are time-tested, tried-and-true methods for achieving the proper atmosphere for quiet and reflective times. With modification these may be used with children who may not possess the requisite know-how to sit quietly and concentrate for sustained periods of time. After these techniques have been practiced a few times with children, the children could be encouraged to employ them anytime they want to reflect on their own.

- Have a pre-established signal for reflection time.

- Use a natural item for the children to focus on, such as a branch, a bowl or pool of water, a plant, a piece of driftwood, or a stone.

- Use a soft voice to give guidelines.

- Sit in a shaded or dimly lit area, outside or inside.

- Remind the children to sit in a comfortable position for reflection and to take a few deep breaths to begin.

- Tell the children that they might find it useful to repeat a phrase or hum one note softly to rid themselves of distracting thoughts as they prepare to reflect.

- You may suggest a topic for reflection or have them choose one of their own.

- To help establish a reflective mood, you may wish to play very quiet music such as George Winston's *December* or Ray Lynch's *Deep Breakfast.*

- Have them reflect in silence for a few minutes.

After a short period of quiet reflection, it is likely that the children's imaginations will be enriched and that they will be more receptive to creative problem-solving activities.

Art, drama, dance, music, and reflection generate and encourage imagination. Incorporate these activities into your gardening program and your boys and girls will be rewarded with an enriched imagination and a creative approach to life.

Literacy

In addition to encouraging creativity, an intent of this book is to develop literacy (reading and writing) skills among children who are gardening. The gardening experience provides children with an experiential foundation or starting point from which to develop the strategies and skills necessary to process written language. A fuller explanation of a methodological sequence an instructor may use to develop experience-based literacy lessons may be found on pages x-xi of *Beyond the Bean Seed.* In addition, there are other ways to help children read a book:

1. Pair them with another child.

2. Read or have the book read to the child.

3. Make a tape recording of the book being read so the child can follow along.

4. Involve the youngsters in literature circles.

Literature circles, according to Harste, Short, and Burke (1988), consist of small groups of children discussing books that all have read. The adult leader encourages discussion by asking a few open-ended questions.

Guidelines for Gardening

If you are just beginning to consider gardening with children, form a support system first. Form a planning committee to seek answers to these questions:

1. Where will the garden be located? It will need:

   at least six hours of sun;

   a conveniently located water source;

   to be out of the way of heavy foot traffic;

   to not replace a popular play area.

2. Who will prepare the site; do the rototilling?

3. Who will garden with the children?

   Consider retired people, Master Gardeners, volunteers, aides, teachers, older teens.

4. What is a reasonable adult-to-child ratio?

5. How will vandalism be prevented?

6. How will the garden be cared for over vacation periods?

7. Where will contributions of seeds, plants, and tools be obtained?

8. How can watering and weeding be kept to a minimum?

9. Will each child have a plot or will everyone work in a large common plot? Will you have a combination of both?

10. How will the produce be divided? Will the children have what they each harvested on a particular day, or will you collect every child's harvest into one common set and then divide it evenly among the children?

11. How will fund raising be handled? Do you need to learn how to write grant proposals?

12. Do you need permission from a governmental agency or private party? How do you get it?

Answers to these and other gardening-with-children questions may be found among these resources:

   Cooperative Extension Agents (county government pages in your phone book)

   Master Gardeners

   Botanical garden personnel

   Garden club members

   Science teachers

And these books:

Bremner, Elizabeth, and John Pusey. *Children's Gardens: A Field Guide for Teachers, Parents, and Volunteers.* University of California Cooperative Extension Common Ground Garden Program, 1990. Information about the availability of this book may be obtained from Common Ground Garden Program, University of California Cooperative Extension, 2615 S. Grand Ave., Suite 400, Los Angeles, CA 90007.

Get Ready, Get Set, GROW. A kit available from the Brooklyn Botanical Gardens, 1000 Washington Ave., Brooklyn, NY 11225.

Jaffe, Roberta. *The Growing Classroom.* Project Life Lab, 1982. Available from Project Life Lab, 809 Bay Ave., Suite H, Capitola, CA 95010.

Ocone, Lynn, with Eve Pranis. *The National Gardening Association Guide to Kids' Gardening.* John Wiley & Sons, 1990. Available from National Gardening Association, 180 Flynn Ave., Burlington, VT 05410.

Tilgner, Linda. *Let's Grow!* Storey Communications, 1988. Available from Storey Communications, Pownal, VT 05261.

Once you have a plan formulated, start digging and reap many benefits for children.

Content and Structure of the Book

Cultivating a Child's Imagination Through Gardening, like its companion book, *Beyond the Bean Seed,* is composed of teaching ideas and suggestions for books related to gardening, creativity, and literacy activities. It is divided into 45 lessons grouped into nine chapters, each containing five lessons. In Chapters 1 and 2 the theme is imagining gardens, their various purposes, and subsequent designs. Children are encouraged to use their imaginations as they dream of a variety of gardens and use various elements of garden design, such as color, line, form, as well as fragrance and texture in order to translate their dreams into actual gardens. Following the guidelines in Chapter 2, the children are encouraged to play with color in the garden.

In Chapters 3 and 4, children are encouraged to imagine and create specialized gardens, many with a particular purpose or theme, such as ancient gardens or craft gardens.

In Chapters 5 and 6, gardeners are asked to think globally as they study how plants and horticultural practices influence politics, economics, and the environment. Teachers will find many tie-ins to social studies and ecology in these chapters.

Chapter 7 introduces gardening readers to the beautiful legends, folktales, and myths created around plants. Instructors seeking ways to incorporate multicultural aspects into their gardening programs will find them here.

Chapters 8 and 9 are about gardeners in fiction and real life. Biographies of famous gardeners, botanists, and naturalists are featured in Chapter 9.

Cultivating a Child's Imagination Through Gardening contains 45 lessons. Each lesson consists of:

A book-sharing time to start each lesson. Because one of the primary goals of this book is to lead children to books by the garden path, all the lessons begin with and are based upon a book. Share the book with your group. You can read the book or parts of the book aloud, showing the illustrations, or telling the story. You may also be able to obtain multiple copies of the book so that your children may enjoy the book on their own during a silent reading time. You may also enlarge the book into a Big Book format so it may be shared at one time with a group. Picture books that have a minimum amount of text adapt well to this method. You may not be able to find the lead book suggested. Use others listed in the "Read More About It" section or in the bibliography at the end of the book. Included with each book entry is a coded reference to the approximate grade level of the book: *P* equals primary, K-3; *P-I* refers to grades 2-4; and *I* refers to intermediate grades 4-6.

A gardening activity based upon the book. This activity may last a few minutes or a few months. For long activities, you will need to remind the students about the book and gardening connection from time to time. It may be appropriate to incorporate the books from the "Read More About It" section during longer projects.

A language arts activity. This may involve speaking, listening, writing, reading, or a combination of some or all. Drama, poetry writing, book compiling, and journal keeping are often featured. When you wish to do this activity is best left up to you and your circumstances. It may best be done at the beginning, middle, or end of the gardening activity.

A creative activity. This may consist of creative thinking, dancing, painting, dramatic productions, puppet making, and party productions. Think how you might incorporate the ideas of Torrance, and Amabile and Tighe, described earlier, in the creative activity.

Most of these activities ask the adult leader to support the children as they reach out to the wider community either for assistance and resources, or to share garden products, knowledge, entertainment, or glad tidings. Sharing and giving away have a way of increasing a positive attitude toward self.

A treat. All the lessons include a treat recipe. Arboretums and botanical gardens that have children's gardening programs contributed some of the recipes, which they offer to both children and volunteers to reward them for their hard work. You may wish to use the treats to express appreciation to the volunteers who have helped your class, group, or club, as well as to brighten the gardening experience among the children.

A poem reference. Nearly every lesson contains a reference to a poem. Please take the time to find the poem or a substitute. Including poetry in each lesson gives your lesson a lift up and out of the grub work. Read the poem aloud to your group and copy it onto a chart for all to read and share. At your local library you will likely find the *Children's Poetry Index*, in which poems are listed by topic. Ask the children's librarian to help you. Be sure to tell him or her what you are doing—connecting children's gardening with children's literature. That way the librarian can be on the lookout for other appropriate poems for you.

Word play. The language of gardening is fun: full of puns, truisms, technical Latin-based vocabulary, wise sayings, metaphors, jokes, and riddles. Thus, gardening language readily lends itself to "Word Play," which is included in most, but not all, lessons.

Supplemental reading. To encourage further reading or to provide you with substitutes for the lead book, a "Read More About It" section is included with each lesson. The books included were chosen for their appropriateness to the lesson and their availability. All were found on the shelves of public and school libraries. Not all libraries will have all the books, so we've listed lots of substitutes. As this book was written, it was easy to observe that libraries everywhere have tight budgets and that most gardening-related books have older copyrights. In defense of those older books, they have some of the best gardening advice, so hang on to them. The newer ones may be prettier but sometimes lack the substance of, say, Katherine Cutler's *The Beginning Gardener*.

Each lesson therefore consists of:

> a book-and its synopsis,
>
> a gardening activity,
>
> a language arts activity,
>
> a creative activity,
>
> a treat,
>
> a poem,
>
> word play, and
>
> a list of supplemental books.

References

Amabile, Teresa, and Elizabeth Tighe. "Questions of Creativity." John Brockman, ed., *Creativity*. New York: Simon & Schuster, 1993.

Harste, Jerome C., Kathy G. Short, and Carolyn L. Burke. *Creating Classrooms for Authors*. Portsmouth, NH: Heinemann, 1988.

Jurenka, Nancy Allen, and Rosanne J. Blass. *Beyond the Bean Seed: Gardening Activities for Grades K-6*. Englewood, CO: Teacher Ideas Press, 1996.

L'Engle, Madeleine. *Walking on Water*. New York: Bantam Books, 1980.

May, Rollo. *The Courage to Create*. New York: Bantam Books, 1975.

Torrance, E. Paul. *The Search for Satori and Creativity*. Buffalo, NY: Creative Education Foundation, 1979.

Chapter 1
DREAMING OF GARDENS

The activities in "Dreaming of Gardens" are intended to involve children in the sequence of imagining what kind of garden the child desires to the nitty-gritty of transforming dreams from graph paper to garden plot. In this chapter children experiment with garden shapes, decide where to site the plot, explore plant choices as they relate to texture and fragrance, and graph garden plans.

This set of lessons should be started in the late winter or early spring when it is still fun to stay indoors and dream of gardens. The unit ends with the children going outdoors to lay out the garden plots they have planned.

1.1 Imagine Your Garden

Burke-Weiner, Kimberly. *The Maybe Garden*. Beyond Words, 1992. 21 pp. (P). Illustrated by Fredrika P. Spillman.

A young boy daydreams while he watches his mother cultivate her garden. From time to time his mom makes a practical suggestion about what he might plant. All her suggestions are met with "Maybe I will." Then the reader is treated to the boy's imaginative alternative. Spillman's vibrant chalk illustrations make this story glow.

Gardening Activity

Imagining Gardens

Say to your group:

What kind of garden do you want, maybe? Here's a chance for you to dream and imagine different kinds of gardens.

A garden does not have to be a 10 x 12-foot plot with neat straight rows of vegetables and a skirt of marigolds. Today we are going to imagine the garden of your dreams. Close your eyes. Follow my directions and use your imagination.

Imagine yourself outdoors. Imagine yourself doing something you really enjoy. [Pause for about 10 seconds to let the imagining occur.] Imagine yourself playing.

Now do something else just as enjoyable. Change and imagine yourself doing another activity. Keep your eyes closed. [Pause for 10 seconds.]

Put yourself in the middle of a large green lawn. Now place a tiny toy on the lawn. Make your toy grow as big as you are. Make it bigger than you are. Change its color. Make it have lights that go on and off. Make the toy as big as the lawn. Now make your toy small again. Imagine that there are 20 toys on the lawn. Imagine yourself going from toy to toy, playing with each one. [Pause.]

Now bring some people you've seen on television to play with you in your yard. Invite some of your friends to join you. Invite some favorite storybook characters to join you. Maybe invite Winnie the Pooh, Raggedy Ann, or Aladdin to join you. Have all these characters and people play one of your favorite games. Now lift yourself way off the ground so you can watch from up above.

Where are your friends, storybook characters, and the television characters playing? Let's make it prettier. All around the lawn put a beautiful flower garden. Color in the flowers. [Pause.] Make the flower garden as big as a playing field. Add some butterflies and hummingbirds. Color them all the colors of the rainbow. [Pause.]

Your friends are tired. They want to sit down. Make them a place to sit. Make it look like an ancient king's throne room. [Pause.]

Now make it all disappear. Come back down to the ground. Imagine yourself surrounded by a sandy desert. What kind of plants can you see? [Pause.] Give yourself a spot to be shaded from the sun. Make it pretty. Make it bigger. Surround your spot with tall trees that have twisted trunks. Put a face on one of the tree trunks. Have it wink at you. [Pause.]

Walk over to the tree trunk. You see teeny tiny gardens in each nook and cranny of the tree trunk. Make each tiny garden different from the others. [Pause.] Make a garden gate appear in the tree trunk. Open it up and walk through it. There's a path. [Pause.] Walk down the path. It leads right back to us. It leads right back to our room. Open your eyes. Stand up. Shake off all the imaginary places. Look around the room. Look at everyone here. You're back from your imaginary trip.

Language Arts Activity

Describing Gardens

Using the ideas of the highly imaginative gardens dreamed of by the young boy in *The Maybe Garden* and by children in the imagination exercise, have your youngsters write a paragraph describing the kind of "Maybe Garden" they would create.

Using drawing paper and the most brilliant crayons, chalk, and markers, have them illustrate their imaginary gardens.

Take time to have the girls and boys share their ideas. Reinforce the notion that when children plan gardens, they need to imagine what they would like to be doing in the garden and what purpose they have for the garden. Remind them that form (the design of the garden) follows function (what the garden will be used for).

Creative Activity

Form Follows Function: Designing Sandbox Gardens

If a sand table or sandbox is available, use it for this activity. Or, use dampened sand spread out on a tarp.

Have available the following materials: a good-sized pile of sand for each child, miniature toys, miniature toy people, toy trains, dried plant material, mirrors, foils, mylar, sponges, artificial turf scraps, plastic, scissors, glue, sticks, and all manner of gadgets and doodads that might come in handy for this activity.

Say to your group, "Form follows function. Design a garden and think first about what you want to do in your garden. Do you want to harvest vegetables? Do you want to play? Do you want to gather big bouquets of flowers? Do you want a place to just sit and take it easy? Do you want to read? Think of what you want to do in your garden. Then create your garden so that will happen."

Have the children play with the materials, creating and re-creating imaginary gardens. The children may want to take photos of their imaginary gardens to preserve their ideas.

Treat

+---
| ### Fantasy Sundaes
|
| Assemble an assortment of ingredients for fantasy sundaes and let the children create their own.
+---

Poem

Prelutsky, Jack. "I Am Growing a Glorious Garden." In *Something Big Has Been Here.* Scholastic, 1990; or Jennings, Elizabeth, "Children at Play." In *Shades of Green.* Greenwillow, 1991.

Word Play

The name of our creative activity is "Form Follows Function," an old saying that artists and architects use. It means that the designer of anything from playgrounds and school buildings to greeting cards and clothing first needs to think of the uses that the place or thing will have before the designer begins to draw the plans for it.

Read More About It

Lovejoy, Sharon. "Plans and Dreams and Garden Schemes." In *Hollyhock Days.* Interweave, 1994. pp. 14-20. (I).

Nash, Ogden. *The Animal Garden.* Evans, 1965. 44 pp. (I).

Spier, Peter. *And So My Garden Grows.* Dell, 1969. 40 pp. (P-I).

Stevenson, James. *Grandpa's Too-Good Garden.* Greenwillow, 1989. 32 pp. (P).

Sutcliff, Rosemary. *Chess-Dream in a Garden.* Candlewick, 1993. 48 pp. (I).

Wiesner, David. *June 29, 1999.* Clarion, 1992. 32 pp. (P-I).

1.2 Where Will Your Garden Grow?

Oechsli, Helen and Kelly Oechsli. *In My Garden: A Child's Gardening Book.*
Macmillan, 1985. 32 pp. (P).
 The authors take the gardening reader step by step through the process of creating
a garden from site selection to planting out the plot. Soft orange, brown, and green
illustrations decorate the pages.

Gardening Activity

Gardener as Decision Maker

 Gardening depends on the gardener's ability to make decisions. How well a garden grows
depends on the planning. A good gardener makes decisions based on analysis of the facts
gathered and coming to appropriate conclusions. Lead your boys and girls through the following
discussion questions:

 We need to decide where to put our garden (or, we need to think about why our garden is
 placed where it is).

 How much sun does a garden need? Where does that happen here? (Have them name several
 places.) What kind of soil does a garden need? Where do we have places with good garden
 soil? What would happen if we placed the garden. . . (name some spots with obvious high
 foot traffic patterns; you want the kids to think by comparison about what happens when
 gardens are sited in harm's way).

 Plants need at least six hours of sunlight, good soil, a spot where they won't be trampled on,
 and what else? Where do we have access to water? What else do we need to think about?
 What else? What else?

 Now, where are the different places for us to put our garden?

 We need to think about what kinds of plants we can grow where we are.

> Where are we?
> What agricultural zone are we in?
> What does that tell us?
> How much rainfall do we get here?
> How much sunshine?
> How much does the wind blow?
> What does that tell us?
> What is our soil like?
> What does that tell us?
> What kinds of insects and other pests do we have?
> What does that tell us?

 Now that we know all that, what can we grow in our garden? What can't we grow? Why?

 Generate a plant list. This may entail having the group browse through seed catalogs to get
more ideas.

Language Arts Activity

Gardeners' Exchange

Have your group contact boys and girls living in various regions of the country. Either by letter or by a computer network such as CompuServe, have them gather information about gardening conditions faced by these other boys and girls. Have your group plan a garden for them based on the information they give you. They might do the following:

Create a plant list.

Provide information about soil amendments, watering schedules, and pest controls.

Share a recipe for plant food.

To exchange ideas with other gardeners, write for copies of *Growing Ideas: A Journal of Garden-Based Learning.* Occasionally this newsletter announces ways that children may share ideas with each other.

> *Growing Ideas*
> National Gardening Association
> 180 Flynn Avenue
> Burlington, VT 05401

Creative Activity

Unusual Garden Sites Mural

Have on hand a large collection of magazines. Create a mural of pictures and photographs of unusual garden sites:

Japanese rice paddy	hotel lobby gardens
terraced hillside	shopping mall gardens
steep, cultivated, rocky hillside	freeway gardens
hanging gardens	tower gardens
desert gardens	water gardens

Treat

All-American Salad

1/4 cup cooked wheat berries (North Central)
1/4 cup cooked, sweetened whole cranberries (Northeast/Northwest)
1 tsp. chopped green chili peppers (Southwest)
1/4 cup chopped jicama (Southwest)
1/2 cup chopped apples (North)
1/4 cup chopped celery (Mid-Atlantic)
1/2 cup cooked wild rice (Central)
1/4 cup chopped peanuts (South)
2 cups cooked brown rice cooked (South and West)
1/4 cup shredded coconut (Hawaii)

Mix together. Pour on your favorite sweet-and-sour dressing. Toss. Serve.

Poem

Fisher, Aileen. "A Garden." In *Always Wondering*. HarperCollins, 1991.

Read More About It

Daddona, Mark. *Hoe, Hoe, Hoe. Watch My Garden Grow.* Addison-Wesley, 1980. 58 pp. (P).

Hershey, Rebecca. *Ready. Set. Grow!* Goodyear, 1995. 104 pp. (P-I).

Ocone, Lynn, with Eve Pranis. *National Gardening Association Guide to Kids' Gardening.* Wiley, 1990. pp. 30-33. (I).

Sunset Editors. *Sunset Best Kids Garden Book.* Sunset, 1992. pp. 17-18. (P-I).

Waters, Marjorie. *The Victory Garden Kids' Book.* Globe Pequot, 1994. pp. 5-12. (I).

1.3 Shapes and Patterns

Rhoades, Diane. *Garden Crafts for Kids: 50 Great Reasons to Get Your Hands Dirty*. Sterling/Lark, 1995. 144 pp. (I).

The perfect book! Just right for children and for those who garden with children. Beautifully formatted, it invites readers to browse through the pages, harvesting idea after idea. Rhoades has written one of the best chapters about designing gardens. Children will discover how to design a garden, the various shapes that gardens may have, and the many considerations that gardeners need to keep in mind as they plan their gardens.

The first six chapters provide detailed directions for establishing, designing, planting, and caring for a garden. Chapter 7 describes dozens of kid-tested, appealing craft ideas, some practical, some decorative, and all doable. Included are toilet-paper seed tape, rustic trellises, shoe scrapers, and worm condos. Recipes are also featured. Apple leather is sure to appeal.

Photographs of children making the projects and working in their gardens clarify the text and inspire replication by children. Bright, attractive, and informative, this book is definitely in the top 10 of current children's gardening books.

Gardening Activity

Shape Gardens

Have on hand art, design, craft, and folk-art books showing such forms as Hmong art, Mexican yarn art, Hawaiian quilt patterns, Ukrainian egg designs, Pennsylvania Dutch designs, Seminole patchwork designs, and the like. Also include garden books that illustrate various garden shapes. Have the children leaf through the books to get ideas for their garden design.

Engage your group in a discussion about the various shapes that gardens may have, for example:

wagon wheel	star
clock	name
rainbow	interlocking circles
ladder	squares or triangles
Asian language symbol	cookie cutter (e.g., gingerbread boy)
American sign language symbols	merry-go-round

Discuss what plants would make the best outline and filler, such as alyssum, marigold, ornamental cabbage, lettuce, miniature zinnia, or coleus.

Have your group plan and plant the garden designs of their choice.

Language Arts Activity

Shape Poems

Like a garden design, poetry may also be shaped. This type is called concrete poetry. Here is an example.

My Pet Flower

```
p         p         p
  e         e         e
    t     t     t
          a l
          s
          t
          e
          m
```

Have the members of your group think of a garden-related topic. Have them think about descriptors as well as how they feel about the topic. Then have them compose shape (concrete) poems about their topics.

Creative Activity

Tangrams

Have your group play around with various designs that can be made with tangrams. Duplicate the tangram pattern provided in figure 1.1 onto tagboard.

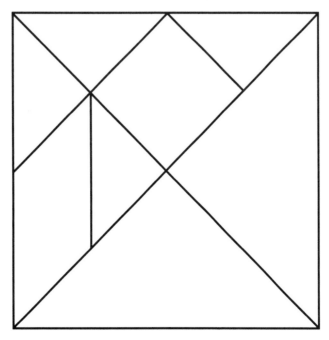

Fig. 1.1. Tangram pattern.

Treat

Shape Cakes

Bake several sheet and one-layer circular cakes. Bring these in and have your boys and girls cut them into squares, rectangles, and half circles. Have them experiment with shapes by rearranging them to form a variety of shapes. When they have one they are satisfied with, frost, decorate, and eat it.

 ## Poem

Froman, Robert. "Undefeated." In *Go with the Poem,* ed. Lilian Moore. McGraw-Hill, 1979.

 ## Word Play

When someone is feeling poorly, he or she says, "I'm in bad shape."
When someone is angry or upset, people may exclaim, "Wow, she sure is bent out of shape."

Read More About It

Campbell, Mary Mason. "The Merry Go Round Garden." In *Kitchen Gardens.* Scribner's, 1971. pp. 138-141. (I-Adult). Illustrated by Tasha Tudor.

Doole, Louise Evans. *Herb Magic and Garden Craft.* Sterling, 1973. pp. 53-60. (I).

Ehlert, Lois. *Color Farm.* Lippincott, 1990. 32 pp. (P).

Lovejoy, Sharon. *Sunflower Houses.* Interweave, 1991. pp. 32-40, 48-51, 56. (I).

Tilgner, Linda. *Let's Grow!* Storey Communications, 1988. pp. 52-61. (I).

Walsh, Anne B. *A Gardening Book.* Atheneum, 1976. pp. 90-97. (I).

1.4 Texture and Fragrance

Sunset Editors. *Sunset Best Kids Garden Book.* Sunset, 1992. 96 pp. (P-I).

This comprehensive garden book covers the basics. If you want to begin a gardening book collection, this should be the first on your list. Boys and girls will learn about gardening tools, planning a garden, starting a worm box, preparing soil, starting plants from seeds, cultivation techniques and house-plant care. For the purpose of this lesson, use page 91 of *Sunset Best Kids Garden Book* for information about plants with texture. Children are encouraged and given directions to plant lamb's ears, scented gernaniums (for their velvety leaves), sea pink, and Irish moss.

Gardening Activity

Touch 'n Sniff Dish Gardens

Have your group investigate which plants are known for fragrance and which are known for the interesting way they feel. Have them create a plant list for each type.

Then have them study the cultivation needs of each so that they can create a dish garden (or window box) of compatible texture and fragrance plants.

You might facilitate this project by bringing in starts of aloe vera, lamb's ears, scented geraniums, thyme, pineapple sage, rosemary, lemon verbena, and mint.

Have the boys and girls pot up compatible plants into dish gardens to be given away to a blind person. The card to the recipient should provide the plant name, care instructions, and directions for transplanting individual plants when they've grown too large. Later, boys and girls may want to work with a local Lions Club to design and plant a garden for the blind in your town.

Language Arts Activity

Braille Alphabet Plant Instructions

Have on hand a copy of the Braille alphabet (fig. 1.2), tagboard, white glue, and pencils.

Say to the group, "On the tagboard write the plant name and care directions in pencil using Braille letter shapes. Use dots of white glue on tagboard to form raised Braille letters after you have printed them out in pencil. Take care not to touch the glue drop until it is very dry."

This may also be done by using bits of aquarium gravel to outline the letters.

Creative Activity

Pomander Balls

Pomander balls are hung in clothes closets to sweeten the air.
Have on hand these materials for each child:

an orange	powdered cinnamon
nylon netting	¼" wide ribbon
2 packages of whole cloves	a fork

Give these directions to your group: Pierce the orange all over with the fork. Insert whole cloves into each hole. Roll the clove-covered orange in powdered cinnamon. Wrap the pomander ball in nylon netting and tie it at the top with ribbon. These make wonderful gifts and/or items to sell for fund-raising.

Braille Alphabet and Numerals

a	b	c	d	e	f	g	h	i	j	k	l	m

n	o	p	q	r	s	t	u	v	w	x	y	z

,	;	:	.	!	(	)	"?	"

Numeral Sign

1	2	3	4	5	6	7	8	9	0

1 ● ● 4
2 ● ● 5
3 ● ● 6

The six dots of Braille are numbered in vertical rows. Dot 6 before a letter indicates a capital.

Fig. 1.2. Braille Alphabet.

Treat

Gingerbread Textured Flowers

1 box gingerbread cookie mix, plus ingredients to prepare
　　dough (per instructions on box)
1 can prepared frosting
Raisins
Chopped nuts

Make a batch of gingerbread cookie dough. Roll out and cut with
floral-shaped cookie cutters. Bake then frost and decorate with
raisins and chopped nuts. You may or may not wish to have
the girls and boys help with this. It depends on your
group and situation.

Poem

Jackson, Kathryn. "Things of Summer." In *Away We Go,* ed. Catherine Schaefer McEwen. Crowell, 1956.

Word Play

A common saying is "That smells as sweet as a rose."
If someone has an irksome personality, we say, "He's as prickly as a cactus."

Read More About It

Cutler, Katherine. *Growing a Garden Indoors or Out.* Lothrop, Lee & Shepard, 1973. 96 pp. (I).

Fell, Derek. *A Kid's First Book of Gardening.* Running Press, 1989. p. 43. (I).

Fenten, D. X. *Plants for Pots.* Lippincott, 1969. pp. 33-41. (I).

Kite, L. Patricia. *Gardening Wizardry for Kids.* Barron's, 1995. pp. 182-213. (P-I).

Lovejoy, Sharon. *Sunflower Houses.* Interweave, 1991. p. 22. (I).

Madgwick, Wendy. *Cacti and Other Succulents.* Steck-Vaughn, 1992. 47 pp. (I).

Tilgner, Linda. *Let's Grow!* Storey Communications, 1988. pp. 103-105. (I).

1.5 Graph Paper Garden Plots

Swenson, Allan. *Big Fun to Grow Book*. McKay, 1977. 170 pp. (I).

A general gardening book, *Big Fun to Grow Book* has the basics and includes a section about planning a garden on graph paper. The contents primarily cover the cultivation of 12 popular flowers and vegetables. Also of note are Swenson's suggestions to older children on how to market their vegetables by setting up their own stand, and how to establish a sales route of customers for their garden produce. No other gardening book for children addresses this issue.

Gardening Activity

Graph Paper Plans

By now gardens have been imagined, molded in sand, and pictured. Now it is time for the children to plan a garden on graph paper and then lay it out in their garden plot after the soil has been prepared.

Keep it simple. The objective here is to have them learn about the value of planning on graph paper. Using a scale of 1 inch per foot and 1-inch graph paper, have your boys and girls plan individual gardens. Have them decide what plants will go where, how long and how wide the rows will be, how wide the walkways will be, and whether or not there will be a border, among other things.

Language Arts Activity

Composition Plans

If graph paper plans provide the structure upon which to design a garden, an outline provides the structure for a written composition.

Have your group members create a short outline that consists of three main sections, each having three subsections, for example:

    I. My garden (write three descriptors of the garden)

        A.

        B.

        C.

   II. Contents of my garden

        A.

        B.

        C.

  III. My garden tasks

        A.

        B.

        C.

Ask the girls and boys to write a three-paragraph composition based on their outline.

Creative Activity

Graph Paper Fantasies

Have on hand graph paper and colored pencils, crayons, or colored pens. The size of the graph paper squares will depend on the developmental level of the boys and girls in your group.

Have the children make lots of designs by filling in the squares as they think best.

When they are finished and all the designs have been shared with the group, ask them how this activity might help them plan more interesting gardens.

Treat

Graph Paper Sandwiches

1 loaf each of unsliced whole wheat and white bread, crusts removed (each loaf must be the same size) Softened butter or margarine.

Slice each loaf lengthwise into six slabs, to make a total of 12 slabs. Butter all the slabs except three of the white ones.

Place the bread into three stacks of four slabs each, starting with a whole wheat buttered one, then a white buttered slab, then whole wheat buttered. The top slab should be a white unbuttered one.

Now slice down into each stack from the top lengthwise (not cross-wise) so that you have six rectangular slabs that reveal white and brown stripes. Butter these rectangular slabs.

Stack these rectangular slabs into four stacks of four, alternating white and whole wheat stripes. You'll have two slices left over to do with as you wish.

The graph paper square pattern should be seen at the end of each loaf. Wrap each loaf in wax paper. Place the loaves into a pan lined with damp paper towels. Cover with a clean cloth towel. Refrigerate. When ready to serve, slice crosswise.

Poem

Fisher, Aileen. "Wise." In *Always Wondering*. HarperCollins, 1991.

Read More About It

Cutler, Katherine N. *Growing a Garden Indoors or Out*. Lothrop, Lee & Shepard, 1973. pp. 18-31. (I).

Fell, Derek. *A Kid's First Book of Gardening*. Running Press, 1989. pp. 19-20. (I).

Ocone, Lynn, with Eve Pranis. *National Gardening Association Guide to Kids' Gardening*. Wiley, 1990. pp. 47-62. (I).

Porter, Wes. *The Garden Book*. Workman, 1989. 64 pp. (I).

Stone, Doris. *A Kid's Guide to Good Gardening*. Brooklyn Botanic Garden, n.d. 45 pp. (P-I).

Chapter 2
DREAMING IN TECHNICOLOR

Boys and girls get to play with color in the garden and the beauty color creates when they do the activities in this chapter. Beginning with a child's favorite color display, the rainbow, the lessons progress to tropical plant colors. Children experiment with color effects and interaction in "Right Color, Right Plant." "Technicolor Vegetables" has children exploring offbeat colors among vegetables. The unit ends with nature's favorite color for plants: green. Holding this variable as a constant, boys and girls experiment with foliage shapes and patterns to produce aesthetically pleasing results.

2.1 Nature's Rainbow-Colored Palette

Ehlert, Lois. *Planting a Rainbow*. Harcourt Brace Jovanovich, 1988. 24 pp. (P).
Bulbs, seeds, and seedlings are selected for the blossoms that will produce rainbow colors. Once all are planted, readers wait for the rainbow to appear in the garden. Ehlert's bold, colorful collages result in a visually stimulating picture book.

Gardening Activity

Rainbow Garden

Plant the plants suggested by Ehlert or have your boys and girls search through seed catalogs to select and order the seeds of colorful plants appropriate for your growing conditions. Design your garden plot in rainbow form and plant accordingly. You may also decide to plant a color-wheel garden to learn more about color with your children.

Language Arts Activity

Rainbow Books

Have on hand these materials: eight pieces of construction paper per child in purple, blue, yellow-green, green, yellow, orange, red, and magenta colors; garden catalogs: glue, multicolored ribbon or yarn; large-eyed needles; hole punch; and scissors.

Have your boys and girls cut out pictures of flowers and vegetables. Have them categorize the pictures by color and glue them onto six of the matching color construction papers. Use the other two for the front and back covers. Have the children write a title on the front cover.

Punch three holes along the left side of each book. Thread a tapestry needle with multicolored ribbon or yarn. Help your boys and girls with these directions:

1. Push the threaded needle down through the middle hole. Leave about 6 inches of ribbon, enough to tie a bow when all is finished.

2. Push the needle up through the top hole.

3. Push the needle down through the bottom hole.

4. Push the needle up through the middle hole.

5. Leave about 6 inches of ribbon. Unthread the needle. Tie the loose ends into a bow.

Creative Activity

Squeegee Rainbows

Either you or a member of your group reads aloud to your group, *A Rainbow of My Own*, by Don Freeman.

Have on hand these materials: yard-long pieces of white mural paper or unglazed, untreated shelf paper for each child; a window-washing squeegee for each child, pair, or small group; a bucket of water; and powdered tempera paint in red, yellow, and blue.

Place the paper on a flat surface, preferably a floor or sidewalk. Instruct the children to sprinkle about a tablespoon each of yellow, then blue, then red tempera paint in the lower left corner of the paper (lower right corner if the child is left-handed).

Have them dip the squeegee into the bucket of water and shake it off so it won't drip. With one big arching swoop they are to swipe over the mural paper with the squeegee, beginning in the lower corner, moving to the top, and ending in the opposite lower corner.

Treat

Rainbows in My Garden Dessert

Prepare a graham cracker crust:
1/4 cup butter, melted
1 cup graham crackers, crushed

Mix butter with graham cracker crumbs. Press into an 8" x 8" baking dish. Refrigerate.

Prepare gelatin cubes:
1 3-ounce package each orange, cherry, and lime gelatin
3 cups boiling water
1 1/2 cups cold water

Mix 1 cup of boiling water and 1/2 cup of cold water with each of the packages of gelatin. Into three separate 8" x 8" pans pour the orange, cherry, and lime gelatin. Chill until firm. When firm, cut into 1/4" cubes (Hint: Dip a sharp knife into hot water after each cut.) Keep refrigerated.

Prepare lemon cream gelatin dessert:
1 cup canned pineapple juce
1/4 cup sugar
1 3-ounce package lemon gelatin
1/2 cup cold water
1 pint frozen nondairy dessert topping

Combine 1 cup canned pineapple juice with 1/4 cup sugar. Heat and stir until the sugar is dissolved. Dissolve lemon gelatin in this hot juice. Add 1/2 cup cold water. Chill until mixture becomes syrupy. Mix the syrupy gelatin with a pint of frozen nondairy dessert topping. Add the cubes of orange, cherry, and lime gelatins. Pour into the prepared crust. Refrigerate 8 hours.

Poem

Merriman, Eve. "Rainbow Writing." In *Rainbow Writing*. Atheneum, 1976.

Read More About It

Bjork, Christina, and Lena Anderson. *Linnea in Monet's Garden*. Raben and Sjorgren, 1978. 53 pp. (P-I).

Cutler, Katherine. *The Beginning Gardener*. Barrow, 1961. 173 pp. (I).

Lovejoy, Sharon. "A Child's Own Rainbow." In *Sunflower Houses*. Interweave, 1991. pp. 50-51. (I).

Lovejoy, Sharon. "I've Got the Blues Garden." In *Hollyhock Days*. Interweave, 1994. pp. 28-29. (I).

Milord, Susan. *The Kids' Nature Book*. Williamson, 1989. p. 49. (I).

2.2 Hawaii Is a Rainbow

Feeney, Stephanie. *Hawaii Is a Rainbow.* University of Hawaii Press, 1988.
60 pp. (P). Photographs by Jeff Reese.

Brilliant full-color photographs of Hawaiian people, places, plants, and animals are arranged according to the colors of the rainbow.

Gardening Activity

Colorful Tropical Plants

Create a tropical rainbow of crotons, bromeliads, sugarcane, and orchids. Crotons have very colorful foliage and bromeliads are excellent companions for orchids.

There are many varieties of orchids, and they come in a rainbow spectrum of colorful blossoms. An orchid genus that is easy to grow, *phalaenopsis,* comes in a wide range of colors. It likes a temperature range of 65 to 85° F and humidity above 50 percent. Critical to its health is moving air; a small fan aimed toward the ceiling helps. It prefers standard orchid potting mix that contains fir bark. Keep moist and well drained.

More information about orchid cultivation may be obtained from:

American Orchid Society
6000 South Olive Avenue
West Palm Beach, FL 33405-4159

Language Arts Activity

An "Our Town Is a Rainbow" Book

Using the photographs taken for the Creative Activity described below, create a bound book. Have the boys and girls write captions for each photograph. Use a variety of colored construction paper for the pages of the book and cut them into a rainbow shape. Title the book *Our Town Is a Rainbow.*

Creative Activity

Rainbows in Our Neighborhood Photos

Hawaii is a rainbow, and so is your neighborhood. Take a walk with a camera and your group of boys and girls around town looking for and photographing plant life that is green, yellow, blue, red, purple, pink, turquoise, orange, lavender, yellow-green, and yellow-orange.

Have the children take close-up photographs of these colorful plants.

Treat

> ## Tropical Fruit Limpias
>
> **Limpias:**
> 1 package eggroll shells (in the supermarket freezer case)
> 2 bananas, cut into tiny chunks
> 1 fresh pineapple, skinned, cored, and cut into tiny
>   chunks (or canned chunks, drained)
> 1 papaya, skinned, seeded, and cut into tiny chunks
>
> 2 Tbs. brown sugar   1 tsp. ground cinnamon
> vegetable oil   1/4 tsp. ground nutmeg
> flour   water
>
> 1. Mix brown sugar and spices. Add to fruits. Stir.
> 2. Place an eggroll wrapper so that the point faces you.
> 3. Place a heaping tablespoon of the spiced fruit pieces in
>   the center of the wrapper.
> 4. Fold two side corners in and roll up like a little dumpling.
>   Seal ends with a mixture of flour and water.
> 5. Repeat until the fruit and/or wrappers are used up.
> 6. Pour 1 inch of vegetable oil into a frying pan and heat it to 375°.
> 7. Place limpias in the pan and lightly fry about 2 minutes
>   or until golden brown.
> 8. Drain well.
> 9. Arrange the fruit limpias on a platter and spoon the
>   haupia sauce (see following recipe) over the limpias.
> 10. Garnish with toasted coconut, chopped macadamia
>   nuts, or fresh berries.
>
> **Haupia Sauce:**
> 1 10-ounce can coconut milk
> 1 cup water
> 1/2 cup granulated sugar
> 2 tsp. cornstarch mixed with 2 tsp. water
>
> Bring the coconut milk, water, and sugar to a light boil; thicken
> with cornstarch mixture; and cook over low heat for 5 minutes.

 Poem

Oram, Hiawyn. *Out of the Blue: Poems About Color.* Hyperion, 1993.

Read More About It

Bown, Deni. *Orchids.* Steck-Vaughn, 1992. 47 pp. (I).

Gibbons, Gail. *Nature's Green Umbrella.* Morrow, 1994. 32 pp. (P-I).

Patent, Dorothy Hinshaw. *Flowers for Everyone.* Dutton, 1990. 64 pp. (I).

Pellowski, Anne. "Why Most Fruit Trees and Plants Have Flat Leaves: A Polynesian Folktale." In *Hidden Stories in Plants.* Macmillan, 1990. 93 pp. (I).

2.3 Right Color, Right Plant

Johnson, Sylvia A. *Roses Red, Violets Blue: Why Flowers Have Colors.* Lerner, 1991. 64 pp. (I).Photographs by Yuko Sato.

One of Johnson's most fascinating books, this gives clear explanations and experiments related to flower pigmentation. Children's vocabularies are guaranteed to expand after an encounter with this book. *Carotene, xanthophylls, anthocyanin, plastid,* and *chromoplast* will become household words.

Gardening Activity

A Color Blanket Garden

Color blanket is a weaver's term for a blanket woven to demonstrate the interaction between various thread colors. Plan and plant a color blanket garden. The garden might be set up in squares in the manner shown here:

	R	**B**	**G**	**Y**	
R	R	R&B	R&G	R&Y	**R**
B	R&B	B	B&G	B&Y	**B**
G	G&R	G&B	G	G&Y	**G**
Y	Y&R	Y&B	Y&G	Y	**Y**
	R	**B**	**G**	**Y**	

R = red salvia
B = blue petunias
G = Bells of Ireland
Y = yellow marigolds

Language Arts Activity

Colorful Flowery Similes

A simile is a figure of speech in which one thing is compared or related to an unlike object or idea. The words *like* and *as* are used in a simile. An example of a simile is "My dog is as playful as a child."

In column form, have your boys and girls list some flowers, fruits, and vegetables and their typical colors. In a third column have them list other objects that are the same in color, for example:

Plant	Color	Another Object
rose	red	fire truck
plum	purple	bruise
carrot	orange	scarf

Have your boys and girls write sentences modeled after this one:

The/my/his/her _____ was as _____ as a _____.

Example: Her scarf was as orange as a carrot.

Creative Activity

Cellophane Flower Pictures

Have on hand these materials: sheets of various colored sheets of cellophane, glue, tagboard frames, clear plastic sheets.

Explore the world of color and color interaction by using various colors of cellophane. Have the children cut flower, fruit, and vegetable shapes from the cellophane. Have them attach these shapes with just a drop of glue in an overlapped fashion to clear plastic that has been attached to a stiff tagboard frame.

Treat

> ## Rainbows in a Glass
>
> Prepare a gelatin treat of three colors: green (lime), orange (orange), and yellow (lemon). Stack layers of prepared gelatin in straight-sided glasses. Be sure to let the first layer congeal before adding the next layer.

Poem

Carlstrom, Nancy White. "Favorite Flower." In *It's About Time, Jesse Bear.* Macmillan, 1990.

Read More About It

Bjork, Christina, and Lena Anderson. *Linnea in Monet's Garden.* Raben and Sjorgren, 1978. 53 pp. (P-I).

Creasy, Rosalind. *Blue Potatoes, Orange Tomatoes.* Sierra Club Books, 1994. 40 pp. (P-I). Illustrated by Ruth Heller.

Ehlert, Lois. *Planting a Rainbow.* Harcourt Brace Jovanovich, 1988. 24 pp. (P).

Evans, David, and Claudette Williams. *Color and Light.* Dorling Kindersley, 1993. 29 pp. (P).

McMillan, Bruce. *Growing Colors.* Lothrop, Lee & Shepard, 1988. 40 pp. (P).

2.4 Technicolor Vegetables

Creasy, Rosalind. *Blue Potatoes, Orange Tomatoes*. Sierra Club Books, 1994. 40 pp. (P-I). Illustrated by Ruth Heller.

Two considerable talents have joined forces to create this entertaining, informative, and colorful book. Rosalind Creasy uses her gardening knowledge to explain how to create a vegetable garden filled with color not ordinarily found there. Ruth Heller's bright illustrations attract children's attention and invite them to learn about vegetables. In addition to practical gardening information, the book contains enticing recipes.

Gardening Activity

Vegetables of a Different Color Garden

Have your group plant vegetables of a different color. More and more are being produced every year. Have your boys and girls peruse seed catalogs to find just the ones right for them. The following are suggestions:

black lettuce	pink popcorn
white pumpkins	burgundy green beans
blue corn	yellow pear tomatoes
white eggplant	chocolate green peppers
yellow watermelon	gold potatoes
lemon cucumbers	easter egg radishes

Companies that carry seed for odd-color vegetables are:

Gurney's	Mellinger's	Henry Fields
110 Capital Street	2310 West South Range Road	415 North Burnett
Yankton, SD 57079	North Lima, OH 44452-9731	Shenandoah, IA 50602

Language Arts Activity

Writing Advertisements

Vegetables of a different color are like new products coming on the market. As such, they need to be sold to a skeptical public. Have your boys and girls select a vegetable to "sell." Have them compare and contrast the new form of the vegetable with the old. Then have them list the advantages of the new color over the old one. Finally, have them write an advertising blurb that persuades folks to buy this new product. Allow them to give their persuasive talk to an audience.

This is an excellent time for a lesson on propaganda techniques, such as snob appeal (only the rich and famous eat burgundy green beans); name-calling (only a dweeb would eat ordinary red tomatoes); glittering generalizations (every boy and girl in Youngstown, Ohio, eats white eggplant); plain folks (the boys at Mel's Auto Body crunch on pink popcorn); testimonial (Susie Superstar says, "I only want chocolate green peppers in my salad"); and bandwagon (join now and get a vegie a month; don't be the last in your neighborhood to join).

Creative Activity

A Let's Be Different Party

Plan and produce a harvest party with your group for the time when you harvest your vegetables of a different color.

At this party all of you will try to be just a little different than you usually are. Introduce the idea of this party by saying, "We are going to have a Let's Be Different Harvesttime Party. We need to discuss how we might do this. What is it about the way a party is usually done that we could change? How could we change the way we dress? How could we change the dances that we usually do? How could we change our faces? What else could be changed?"

Allow them to carry out their plans so long as they are reasonable, appropriate, and safe, yet still keep the notion of celebrating differences. At the party you might create a new dance in honor of a vegetable (the pink popcorn bop), dress in T-shirts dyed in vegetable colors, paint faces, and of course eat your vegetables.

Be sure to play the "Guess the Vegie" games as described by Jane Taylor in her treat recipe, which follows.

Treat

4-H Children's Garden Grab Bag Dip

2 cups mayonnaise
1/4 cup freshly
  grated horseradish
1/2 tsp. salt

1/2 cup sour cream
2 Tbs. dry mustard
1 Tbs. lemon juice

Mix everything together in a large bowl. Add chopped vegetables of a different color from your garden. Supply large toothpicks, fondue forks, or kabob sticks. Have the boys and girls stab and name a vegetable from the grab bag dip.

(Modifed from the recipe supplied by Jane Taylor, Curator, Michigan 4-H Children's Garden, Michigan State University, East Lansing, Michigan. This extensive garden is open to the public and visitors are welcome.)

Poem

Rieu, E.V. "The Paint Box." In *The Oxford Treasury of Children's Poems,* by Michael Harrison and Christopher Stuart-Clark. Oxford University Press, 1988.

Word Play

Usually we say of embarrassed persons that their faces are beet red. Now what shall we say?

Read More About It

Fell, Derek. *A Kid's Book of Gardening.* Running Press, 1989. pp. 55-57. (I).

Johnson, Sylvia A. *Roses Red, Violets Blue.* Lerner, 1991. 64 pp. (I). Photographs by Yuko Sato.

McMillan, Bruce. *Growing Colors.* Lothrop, Lee & Shepard, 1988. 40 pp. (P).

2.5 Green Foliage Gardens

Harvey, Anne. *Shades of Green*. Greenwillow, 1991. 192 pp. (P-I).

A collection of poems that celebrate nature, gardens and gardening, seasons, and cities, this book reflects many moods—from anger to nostalgia to celebration. There's a poem for nearly every event, season, and feeling known to gardeners.

Gardening Activity

Leafy Gardens

Explore and experiment with plants that show off with leaves rather than flowers. This is an appropriate time to explore artemisia, coleus, dusty miller, Mexican firebush, hostas, caladiums, ferns, kale, elephant ears, lady's mantle, and sedum. If possible, obtain potted-up specimens from a local nursery so the plants can be moved around to find the most pleasing arrangements.

Leaf shape, size, and texture need to be noted and discussed with your group. Have your boys and girls experiment with groupings that contrast solid, spiky, feathery, palmate, lobed, and split foliage. Draw their attention to round, oval, airy, large, and small leaves. Discuss each of the groupings in terms of the following:

What is the most pleasing arrangement? Why?

What is the least? Why?

Are a variety of shapes more pleasing than the same shape?

What plants are best used as a massed background?

What plants are best used as an accent?

What happens when we place a round-leafed plant in juxtaposition to a narrow-spiked leaf plant?

What is the proportion to have?

Finally, design and plant a foliage garden.

As an alternative, gather a variety of houseplants and have the members of your group experiment with grouping them in the most pleasing, contrastive placements.

Language Arts Activity

Science Experiment Notebook

Leaves are important to the life of a plant. While the focus is on foliage, this is an appropriate time to study chlorophyll. Have your boys and girls do the standard experiment to prove the function of chlorophyll. Obtain two healthy specimens of the same plant variety, say, two bean or geranium plants. Have your boys and girls place one in a closet or cabinet where it will receive no sunlight. Place the other in a sunny window. Water each the same amount. Have the children keep notes about what happens over time. Duplicate the experiment form (fig. 2.1). Have as many copies as the number of children multiplied by the number of days you think the experiment will take, say, a week. The form will support the boys and girls by providing a structure within which to write.

Science Experiment Form

Name _____

On _____ Plant A was _____
         (date)   (Tell what happened to it.)

_____

It received _____ of water.
                   (how much)

It received _____ of sunlight.
                  (how many hours)

It looked _____ because _____
    (Describe its condition.)   (Speculate about the reasons.)

This may prove that _____

_____

On _____ Plant B was _____
         (date)   (Tell what happened to it.)

_____

It received _____ of water.
                   (how much)

It received _____ of sunlight.
                  (how many hours)

It looked _____ because _____
    (Describe its condition.)   (Speculate about the reasons.)

This may prove that _____

_____

Fig. 2.1. Science Experiment Form.

From *Cultivating a Child's Imagination Through Gardening.* © 1996. Nancy Allen Jurenka and Rosanne J. Blass. Teacher Ideas Press. (800) 237-6124.

Have your boys and girls compile these notes into a bound notebook. Discuss their observations as a group. Ask what happened. Why did it happen? Depending on their reading level, read aloud to them or have them read silently information about chlorophyll and photosynthesis from *How Nature Works* by David Burnie.

Creative Activity

Foliage Waste Baskets

Obtain empty gallon ice cream containers from your local ice cream store. Have on hand white, untreated, unglazed shelf paper or white mural paper; self-polishing liquid floor wax; white glue; paintbrushes (disposable foam ones are recommended); and rickrack (from a fabric store).

Have the children wash out the ice cream containers. Have the children collect a variety of leaves (small fern fronds are ideal). Then have them arrange and glue the leaves in an attractive pattern on the white paper that has been cut to fit around the ice cream containers. Finally, have them glue the decorated shelf paper onto the ice cream container. Be sure all leaf parts are glued down flat. Then have the children paint the leaves and the shelf paper with liquid floor wax. Allow to dry.

Treat

Crystallized Mint Leaves

Have on hand washed mint leaves, stiffly beaten egg white, oil of peppermint or spearmint, and fine sugar. Brush each leaf with the egg white. Dip the leaf into sugar that has been flavored with a drop of mint oil. Cover with waxed paper. Bake in a 250° F oven until dry.

Poem

Adoff, Arnold. *Greens.* Lothrop, Lee & Shepard, 1988.

Word Play

When someone says, "I need some green stuff," they mean that they need paper money. When someone wants something another person has, he or she may say, "I'm green with envy." *Greens* is another word for lettuce, beet leaves, dandelion, and turnip leaves.

Read More About It

Buki, Ltd. *Our Garden.* Buki Toys, 1992. (P-I).

Katz, Adrienne. *Naturewatch.* Addison-Wesley, 1986. pp. 84-85 (I).

Kite, L. Patricia. *Gardening Wizardry for Kids.* Barron's, 1995. pp. 132-33. (P-I). Illustrated by Yvette Santiago Banek.

Kramer, Jack. *Plant Sculptures.* Morrow, 1978. 63 pp. (I).

Lubell, Winifred, and Cecil Lubell. *Green Is for Growing.* Rand McNally, 1964. 64 pp. (P-I).

Millard, Adele. "Foliage Plants." In *Plants for Kids.* Sterling, 1975. pp. 83-94. (I).

Wexler, Jerome. *From Spore to Spore.* Dodd, Mead, 1985. 48 pp. (P-I).

Chapter 3
SPECIALTY GARDENS

For groups who desire more than the basic garden, this chapter provides variations. Included here is an examination of the great variety of thematic gardens. Also included are "Ancient Gardens," "Herb Gardens," "Prehistoric Gardens," and "Native American Gardens." All the activities in this set of lessons are best done during the growing season.

Leaders and teachers seeking connections to social studies will find numerous ones in this chapter.

3.1 Thematic Gardens

Lovejoy, Sharon. *Hollyhock Days.* Interweave, 1994. 95 pp. (I).

In this sequel to *Sunflower Houses,* Sharon Lovejoy, garden writer and owner of Heart's Ease Herb Shop and Gardens, goes well beyond the bean-seed level of children's gardening. Readers will want to try planting gardens to attract caterpillars, planting a hollyhock tent, or planning and designing an "I've-Got-the-Blues" garden. Other ideas for thematic gardens can be found in *Sunflower Houses.* Both convey the aesthetic value of gardening as well as the playfulness and soul-satisfying pleasure of it.

Gardening Activity

The Science Education Garden

Some folks believe the primary function of a children's garden is to teach science. To facilitate that notion, one could design and plant a garden around the needs of science activities. Here are some ideas:

Plant	Science Activity
tulips or poppies	Flower parts can be easily seen and identified.
sunflowers	Seed production from bud to flower to seed is easily observable.
lima-bean seeds	The germination process is easily observed.
squash	Male and female flowers and their differences are readily seen.
ferns	Reproduction by spores can be observed.
red salvia	Plants with the right color increase their chances of being reproduced by attracting pollinators.
spider plants	Some plants reproduce by runners.
potatoes	Demonstrate plant parts, including tubers.
alpines	Plants grow under a variety of conditions, including mountainous.
cacti	Plants can retain moisture and survive under drought or desert conditions.
morning glories	Some plants are influenced by the sun and demonstrate heliotropism.
potted plants	Photosynthesis and the function of chlorophyll can be demonstrated using a dark closet.
Queen Anne's lace, celery, carnations	How a plant moves water and food (osmosis) can be demonstrated using food coloring.
Hops, sweet peas, chamomile, parsley, aristolochia, bronze fennel	Attract butterflies; caterpillars can be observed.

Plant a garden with these plants, and object lessons for science education will be right at hand. You will have a garden of "teachable moments."

Language Arts Activity

Webs in the Garden—Thematic Projects

A thematic garden can be used as a springboard to other areas of study and activity that may be synthesized into reports, projects, and programs. The variety of choices among themes are numerous. Following are some examples:

Colonial	Pizza	Prehistoric
Medicinal Herbs	Fabric	Peter Rabbit
Butterfly	Native Plants	Specific Colors
Dye Plants	Little House	Biblical
Shakespeare	Great Grandmother's	Mint
Tasha Tudor	Clock	Four Seasons
Desert	Dixie	Tropical
Water	Rainbow	50 States
Mediterranean	Asian	Model Railroad
Soap and Sponge	Tea	Edible Flowers
Bird Feeders	Alaskan	Night Bloomers
Gertrude Jekyll	Celia Thaxter	Toys
Out of Africa	Out of India	Out of Mexico
Christmas	Halloween	St. Patrick's Day
For the Handicapped	Full o' Flavor	Perfumer's
Flower Arrangers	Alphabet	Native American
	Just for Cats	Dutch

Having planted a thematic garden, how can you translate the theme into projects, activities, and programs? A good way to begin is with a semantic map, which helps children brainstorm and think divergently while keeping them focused on the theme. Typically, in an instructional situation, the topics to which the theme is related can be connected to those in an elementary school curriculum. The example given here revolves around Thomas Jefferson's garden (see fig. 3.1).

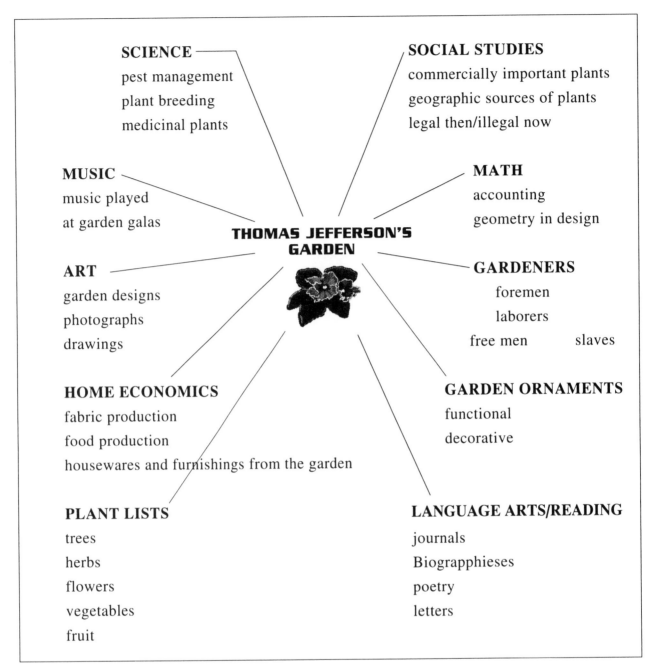

Fig. 3.1. Semantic map of Thomas Jefferson's garden.

After the children generate such a web by lengthy discussion, research topics are chosen by individuals, pairs, and small groups. After they have read widely on their topics, searched for appropriate audiovisual materials, taken notes, written an outline, and written their reports, the children need to decide how they wish to present this material and to whom they wish to present it. This process may take up to four weeks for themes as complex as Thomas Jefferson's Garden, or a few days in the case of Pizza Gardens. The program could be a panel discussion with audiovisual embellishments or an opera.

Creative Activity

Crafts from the Craft Child's Garden

Grow it and make it! In a garden created just for children who enjoy crafts, you may find plants that lend themselves to projects. Here are some suggestions:

Plant	Use
wheat and grasses	plaiting, braiding, coiling, weaving
gourds	birdhouses, bowls, ornaments
pumpkins	carving, 3-D sculptures
dainty flowers	pressing, laminating
statice and everlastings	wreaths and swags
grapevines and willows	weaving, coiling; baskets, furniture
corn	dolls and ornaments
lavender	sachets
catnip	cat toys
cotton	spinning
yucca	weaving
cut flowers	flower arrangements

Treat

Spearmint Ices from the Mint Garden

Master Gardeners in Kittitas County, Washington, served this treat at the county fair.

2 cups sugar
5 cups water
shaved ice

1/4 cup chopped fresh spearmint leaves
Spearmint sprigs

Make a simple syrup by combining the sugar with the water and spearmint leaves. Bring to a boil. Reduce heat and simmer for 5 minutes. Cool and refrigerate overnight. Strain. Fill paper cups with shaved ice. Pour the mint syrup over the ice. Top with a spearmint sprig.

Poem

McCord, David. "Mr. Bidery's Spidery Garden." In *The Random House Book of Poetry for Children,* ed. Jack Prelutsky. Random House, 1983. p. 34.

Read More About It

Garland, Sarah. *Peter Rabbit's Gardening Book.* Warne, 1983. 48 pp. (P-I).

Lovejoy, Sharon. *Sunflower Houses.* Interweave, 1991. 144 pp. (I).

Marshall, Virginia Stone. *Flower Arranging for Juniors.* Little, Brown, 1954. 113 pp. (I).

Sedenko, Jerry. *The Butterfly Garden.* Villard, 1991. 144 pp. (I)

Wilbur, C. Keith. *Indian Handcrafts.* Globe Pequot, 1990. 144 pp. (I).

3.2 Ancient Gardens and Stories

Paterson, John, and Katherine Paterson. *Consider the Lilies.* Crowell, 1986. 96 pp. (I). Illustrated by Anne Ophelia Dowden.

Beautifully illustrated by Anne Ophelia Dowden, the book is a series of biblical vignettes accompanied by anecdotes about the plants mentioned. The history and lore of plants growing in Israel now and in biblical times are included. For example, the reader learns of the lentils eaten by Esau, the castor-bean plant under which Jonah sat, and the wheat and tares of the parables. The symbolism, significance, and use of plants by ancient populations are explained.

A resource book of ethnobotony and plant lore written and illustrated by prize-winners, this book is a valuable reference.

Gardening Activity

Ancient Garden

The most obvious activity would be designing and planting a biblical garden; however, space and situational constraints may not permit this in full. In a public school situation, children could plant an Ancient Times and Ancient Stories Garden. This would be especially appropriate if ancient civilizations were being studied in social studies classes.

Most plants mentioned are trees, shrubs, and plants that grow well in a warm Mediterranean climate, which places limitations on growing a complete garden of the plants mentioned in the book. Plants that could be grown in a single growing season are wheat, mustard, barley, corn poppies, artemisia, anemone, rock roses, and the castor-bean plant. Also possible would be iris, Madonna lilies, crocus, and narcissus. A cautionary note: The seeds of the castor-bean plant are poisonous.

Create a small garden of these plants, and tell their stories during a presentation program or garden tour.

Language Arts Activity

Stories in the Ancient Tradition

Stories of old often celebrated human virtues. What are virtues? They are human qualities such as bravery, honesty, thriftiness, hard work, kindness, tenacity, cheerfulness, and generosity. In addition, plants have long been the subject of parables, fables, folktales, and legends. Read aloud some parables or fables to your group, for example, Anne Pellowski's *Hidden Stories in Plants.*

Have your boys and girls write their own parables in which plants are the characters. To engage the children in "prewriting thinking," have them consider the qualities of selected flowers or plants. Next, brainstorm about metaphors and similes to help get creativity flowing. For instance, you might model this behavior by getting them to think of various ways to fill in these blanks:

```
_____ is as _____ as a rose.
Example: Sue's kindness is as beautiful as a rose.

_____ is as _____ as a daisy.
Kerry is as cheerful as a daisy.
```

```
_____ is as _____ as a cactus.
Lars is as full of prickers as a cactus.

_____ is as _____ as a pumpkin vine.
Sue's thinking is as twisted as a pumpkin vine.
```

Then move to beginning lines or story starters, for example:

```
    Once there was a daisy growing by a pig's pen. The
pig _____
```

Then help the writers think about how the story might continue. Finally, a "think about it question" such as, What lesson about life could the pig learn from the daisy?

An ancient story starter might be:

```
    Once there was a cactus that grew near a coyote's den.
The coyote pup _____
```

Think-about-it-questions:

What kind of personality will the cactus have in your story?

What kind of behaviors will you give the coyote pup?

What lesson about one of the virtues could the cactus teach the coyote?

Another ancient story starter might be:

```
    Once there was a morning glory vine growing near a sun-
flower. The morning glory vine _____.
```

Think-about-it questions:

What qualities will you give to the morning glory?

What behaviors will you have the sunflower show?

What could the morning glory vine learn from the sunflower?

After these short conversations, allow your children time to complete their ancient plant parables.

After the fables and parables have been drafted and edited, they can be placed in a class book or posted on a bulletin board. For younger children, simply read aloud stories from Anne Pellowski's *Hidden Stories in Plants*.

Creative Activity

Making a Wheat Swag

Have on hand these materials: 26 large-headed, pliable wheat stalks; cotton thread; and ribbon. Procedure:

1. Tie three long wheat stalks together underneath their heads with cotton thread.

2. Bend two of the stalks so that one points east and the other west.

3. Bend the right-hand stalk over the center stalk, just as one would do when plaiting hair.

4. Bring the left-hand stalk over between the center stalk and the right-hand stalk. Keep repeating this process until you have a 7" braid.

5. Repeat using three more wheat stalks. Now you should have two 7" braids of wheat stalks. Set them aside.

6. Gather a sheaf of 20 wheat stalks.

7. Tie these 20 into a bundle underneath their necks (under the stalk head). Think of this tie as Tie A.

8. Tie this bundle at a second point 3" below the first tie. Think of this tie as Tie B.

9. With string, thread, or raffia, attach the two braids at Tie B on either side of the bundle.

10. Bend the braids into a heart shape.

11. Tie the other ends of the braids together to the bundle at Tie A.

12. Embellish with ribbon and dried flowers.

Treat

Ancient Stories Menu and Recipe

Grape Juice	Whole Wheat Pita Bread
Olives	Almonds, Dates, and Figs
Red Lentil Stew	

———————— **Red Lentil Stew** ———— ——

1 Tbs. oil	1 cup of dry red lentils
1 onion, chopped	salt and pepper to taste

Over medium heat, cook the chopped onion in oil until transparent. Raise the heat and cook until golden brown. Take care not to let the onion burn. Lower the heat. Add the lentils and just enough water to cover. Simmer until the lentils are tender, about 30 minutes. Puree or mash the lentils so you have a thick stew. Return them to the pan. Add just enough salt and pepper to bring out the flavor.

Poem

Guiterman, Arthur. "Ancient History." In *The Oxford Book of Children's Verse in America*, by Donald Hall. Oxford University Press, 1985.

Read More About It

Conaway, Judith. *City Crafts from Secret Cities*. Follett, 1978. 96 pp. (I).

Johnson, Sylvia. *Wheat*. Lerner, 1990. 48 pp. (I).

Kite, L. Patricia. *Gardening Wizardry for Kids*. Barron's, 1995. 220 pp. (P-I). Illustrated by Yvette Santiago Banek.

Lerner, Carol. *A Biblical Garden*. Morrow, 1982. 48 pp. (I).

Limburg, Peter. *What's in the Name of Flowers*. Coward, McCann & Geoghegan, 1974. 190 pp. (I).

Pellowski, Anne. *Hidden Stories in Plants*. Macmillan 1990. 93 pp. (I).

Selsam, Millicent, and Jerome Wexler. *Eat the Fruit, Plant the Seed*. Morrow, 1980. 48 pp. (P-I).

3.3 Herb Gardens

Verey, Rosemary. *The Herb Growing Book.* Little, Brown, 1980. 41 pp. (I).

Verey explains the culture requirements of a variety of herbs, how to design, plan, and plant an herb garden. She also describes crafts such as potpourri and tussie-mussies and gives directions for making tisanes (teas), including rose hip tea.

Gardening Activity

Growing Herbs Inside and Outside

The seven herbs most successfully grown indoors are basil, chives, thyme, sage, parsley, marjoram, and rose geranium. If you have GrowLab (from the National Gardening Association), a lighted plant stand, or a sunny window, grow these herbs in pots with your group. If it is late spring when you are making herb gardening plans, you might like to plant spearmint and lavender seedlings outdoors. These are useful for projects later in the summer. Your boys and girls may also enjoy growing that tasty pizza herb, oregano.

Language Arts Activity

Tussie-Mussies; or, The Language of Flowers

Tussie-mussies are nosegays or small bouquets of herbs and flowers. People living in Victorian times gave each flower in their tussie-mussie a meaning. Since then the tradition has been that herbs have a language that speaks of qualities. Using herbs found in your group's and neighborhood gardens, have the boys and girls prepare tussie-mussies to give to community service people to express appreciation for the work they do. Following are some herbs and their traditional meanings:

aloe—shelter from harm	fennel—power and endurance
angelica—inspiration	goldenrod—encouragement
basil—good wishes	iris—courage
bay—achievement	lady's mantle—protection
borage—bravery	mugwort—pleasant journeys
chamomile—wisdom or fortitude	sage—wisdom
chervil—sincerity	savory—interest
chives—usefulness	scented geranium—happiness
costmary—sweetness	southernwood—constancy
dill—survival	

A tussie-mussie of lady's mantle, basil, borage, dill, and iris might be given to a policeman or -woman. For a postal worker, include mugwort, goldenrod, southernwood, chives, and fennel. For a librarian, put together a bouquet of angelica, bay, chamomile, chervil, costmary, scented geranium, sage, and savory. What would firemen and -women appreciate? Be sure your boys and girls include a note that provides a glossary of herb language.

Creative Activity

Lavender Wands

Have on hand these materials:

13 stalks of lavender
three yards of 1/4" ribbon
a tapestry needle.

Tie the bunch of lavender stalks together just below the flower heads. Bring the bottom end of each stalk up and over the bundled flower heads so they look as though they are in a cage. Beginning at the top, weave the ribbon in, out, and around the lavender flower heads until they are completely enclosed. Tie a bow underneath the flower heads. The stalks serve as a handle for the wand.

Treat

> ## Herb Spread
>
> Boys and girls who garden at the Fort Worth Botanic Garden like to mix garlic, chives, basil, and oregano with cream cheese that they spread on crackers for a treat.

Poem

Herb Gardens Enchant
On warm summer days thyme and lavender
perfume the air; hummingbirds linger; and the silvery-down
of lamb's ears invites your soft caress.

—Anonymous

Read More About It

Bown, Deni. *Growing Herbs.* Dorling Kindersley, 1995. 80 pp. (I).

Bradstreet, Brenda. *The Compact Herb Garden.* Solly's Choice, 1991.

Doole, Louise Evans. *Herb Magic and Garden Craft.* Sterling, 1973. 192 pp. (I).

Dowden, Anne Ophelia. *This Noble Feast.* Collins, 1979. 80 pp. (I).

Furlong, Monica. *Wise Child.* Knopf, 1987. 228 pp. (I).

Gianni, Enzo. *Little Parsley.* Simon & Schuster, 1990. 32 pp. (P).

Kite, L. Patricia. *Gardening Wizardry for Kids.* Barron's, 1995. pp. 150-81. (P-I). Illustrated by Yvette Santiago Banek.

Lavine, Sigmund. *Wonders of Herbs.* Dodd, Mead, 1976. 64 pp. (I).

Pallotta, Jerry. *The Spice Alphabet Book.* Charlesbridge, 1994. 32 pp. (P-I). Illustrated by Leslie Evans.

Powell, E. Sandy. *A Chance to Grow.* Carolrhoda, 1992. 36 pp. (P-I). Illustrated by Zulma Davila.

3.4 Prehistoric Gardens

Center for Science in the Public Interest. Project Inside/Outside. *Ladybugs and Lettuce Leaves*. Center for the Study of Science in the Public Interest, 1982. 84 pp. (I).

A description of prehistoric plant evolution is included in this guide to gardening and environmental science. The authors also provide basic gardening directions and activities relating to plants. The book enables young people to make informed decisions about siting the garden, improving soil, and selecting seeds. Black-and-white photos and line drawings supplement the text.

Gardening Activity

Design

Using graph paper, design a prehistoric landscape of plant life.

Language Arts Activity

Research, List, and Describe

Research, list, and describe early plant life from prehistoric times and the age of dinosaurs.

Creative Activity

Diorama

Create a shoebox (or larger) diorama depicting prehistoric plant and animal life. Use your research from the Language Arts Activity to help prepare the diorama. Consider what plants exist today that resemble prehistoric plants.

Treat

Prehistoric Trees

1 carrot
1 green pepper
cream cheese with chives

Wash carrot and green pepper. Put a large dab of cream cheese in the center of a small paper plate. Stand the carrot upright on the cream cheese. Place another dab of cream cheese on top of the carrot. Remove the core and seeds from the green pepper. Cut the edges of the green pepper to resemble a jagged umbrella or a palm tree. Place green pepper on top of the carrot. Anchor with more cream cheese if necessary.

Poem

Norris, Leslie. "The Black Fern." In *The Scott, Foresman Anthology of Children's Literature,* by Zena Sutherland and Myra Cohn Livingston. Scott, Foresman, 1984.

Read More About It

Donnelly, Liza. *Dinosaur Garden.* Scholastic, 1990. 32 pp. (P).

Henderson, Douglas. *Dinosaur Tree.* Bradbury, 1994. 32 pp. (P-I).

Sterling, Dorothy. *The Story of Mosses, Ferns, and Mushrooms.* Doubleday, 1955. 159 pp. (I).

Wexler, Jerome. *From Spore to Spore.* Dodd, Mead, 1985. 48 pp. (P-I).

3.5 Native Gardens

Caduto, Michael, and Joseph Bruchac. *Native American Gardening*. Fulcrum Publishing, 1996. 158 pp. (I-Adult).

Well researched and thoughtfully written, *Native American Gardening* describes gardeing in terms of a spiritual activity in which gardeners gain respect for the circle of life. Native North American gardening practices, stories, crafts, customs, and recipes are shared by two well-respected native folklorists and storytellers. Explicit directions are given for designing, planting, and maintaining a Three Sisters Garden in addition to detailed directions for gourd cultivation and crafts. Respect for the seed and its care is emphasized. This book is a gardening social studies teacher's dream come true. Those parents, youth leaders, and teachers searching for an integrating way to teach ecology will find it in this balanced work.

Gardening Activity

Plant a Seneca Garden

The Seneca Indians always plant corn, squash, and beans (the Three Sisters) together. Plant a Seneca garden. On a calendar with large squares, jot down daily observations on how your garden is progressing. Take weekly photographs to document the progress of your garden. Date each picture and write a brief caption on the back. Keep a journal on the growth, care, and harvesting of your garden. Did the corn, squash, and beans in your garden grow the same way that was described in the book? Why or why not?

Language Arts Activity

Native Legends

While some Native Americans of the eastern and southwestern United States did cultivate crops, others such as the Plains Indians were hunters and gatherers from Mother Nature's garden. Collect Native American legends of plants and plant materials. You may wish to begin with the book *Song of the Seven Herbs*, by Walking Night Bear and Stan Padilla.

Creative Activity

Native Dyes

Alder roots, bloodroot roots, grapes, oak bark, and sunflowers were commonly used by Native Americans to dye goods. Directions and recipes for gathering and using vegetable dyes can be found in *Vegetable Dyes* by Douglas Leechman.

Treat

Sunflower Seeds

Serve sunflower seeds.

 Poem

Pomerantz, Charlotte. "Where Do These Words Come From?" In *Sing a Song of Popcorn,* ed. Beatrice S. De Regniers. Scholastic, 1988.

Read More About It

Guidetti, Geri. *A Seneca Garden.* KMG Publications, 1980. 24 pp. (I).

Hughes, Monica. *A Handful of Seeds.* Lester Publishing, 1993. 32 pp. (P-I).

Leechman, Douglas. *Vegetable Dyes.* Webb, 1945. 55 pp. (I-Adult).

Lucas, Jannette May. *Indian Harvest.* Lippincott, 1985. 118 pp. (I).

Mamchur, Carolyn Marie, with Meguido Zola. *In the Garden.* Pemmican Publications, 1993. 48 pp. (P-I).

Walking Night Bear and Stan Padilla. *Song of the Seven Herbs.* Book Publishing Company, 1987. 60 pp. (I).

Wilbur, C. Keith. *Indian Handcrafts.* Globe Pequot, 1990. 144 pp. (I).

Wilson, Gilbert L. *Buffalo Bird Woman's Garden.* Minnesota Historical Society, 1987. 129 pp. (I-Adult).

Wittstock, Laura Waterman. *Ininatig's Gift of Sugar.* Lerner, 1993. 48 pp. (I).

Chapter 4
VEGETABLE GARDENS

The books and activities in this chapter showcase the fun and variety to be found among certain classes of vegetables. Children are encouraged to try their hand at growing plants of different sizes, from miniature pumpkins to skyscraper corn.

The lead books provide variety in children's literature also. A retold Russian folktale, *The Turnip,* enriches the experience of growing root vegetables. Hannah Johnson's photo-essay stimulates children's interest in growing a salad garden. The whimsical *Gardening with Peter Rabbit* encourages children to get an early start with gardening. This activity would be well done during early spring so classroom teachers looking for a gardening activity to complete before school is finished will appretiate the "Easy and Early Vegetables" lesson.

Sharon Lovejoy has written an inspiring and nostalgic work in which she encourages gardeners to experiment with a variety of vegetables, including miniatures. For a chuckle, children will enjoy *Grandpa's Too-Good Garden,* a cartoonlike picture book by humorist James Stevenson. This book could be read just before planting giant pumpkin seeds or after the skyscraper corn has been harvested.

4.1 Underground Gardens

de la Mare, Walter. *The Turnip*. Godine, 1992. 32 pp. (I). Illustrated by Kevin Hawkes.

Once there were two half-brothers: one known for his generosity, the other for his meanness. After feeding a strange old man, the generous half-brother finds an enormous turnip on his farm. He takes the turnip to the king and is rewarded well. The selfish half-brother is determined to give the king a gift in hopes of receiving a valuable gift. The king, aware of the mean half-brother's reputation, gives him a well-deserved but surprising reward.

Gardening Activity

Underground Vegie Contest

Have your group plant carrots, beets, turnips, parsnips, rutabagas—one, some, or all. Be certain to remind the children that these are called root vegetables.

You may wish to divide your group into teams that will plant experimental plots to see which team can grow:

> the biggest
>
> the funniest-looking
>
> the straightest
>
> the most crooked
>
> the best-tasting root

Language Arts Activity

Underground Press

In tabloid format, create a newspaper edition devoted to root or underground vegetables. Have the group create either a straightforward newspaper with news, feature articles, vegetable jokes, crossword puzzles, sports, fashion, and homemaking sections or a parody of *National Enquirer* types of papers with humorous, exaggerated articles about the life and times of famous underground vegetables. Be sure to include a vegie-ological column in which forecasts are made about people born at certain periods of time. Substitute vegetable names for astrological ones. Have fun. Be certain to include a gossipy story about the turnip that was featured in the lead book.

Creative Activity

Decorative Vegies

A few weeks before doing the activity described below, have your group prepare a turnip centerpiece: Slice a sliver from the bottom of a turnip so it will sit flat. Hollow out the turnip (not so much that it collapses). Fill the hollow with soil. Plant grass seed. Keep the soil moist. Set the turnip in indirect sunlight. When the grass seed has sprouted, fashion facial features for the turnip with pieces of other underground vegetables. Use toothpicks to attach eyes, nose, ears, and mouth cut from these vegetables.

Turnips, carrots, beets, jicama, and radishes lend themselves to creative slicing, dicing, and shaping. Have your group create decorative vegetable garnishes. To be on the safe side, make sure the children have washed their hands and allow them to use canape cutters and vegetable slicers. You should help out with a sharp knife as needed. Have them soak thin slivers of carrot in ice water so they will curl.

In the center of a serving piece (depending on how you choose to use this project, could be a paper plate or a china platter), place the decorated, grassy-haired turnip. Surround the turnip with an attractive arrangement of the other vegetable garnishes. Either use the garnishes for your treat or give the decorative arrangement to a friend of the group. ("Friend" may be broadly defined: a shut-in, the folks at a homeless shelter, a Sunday school teacher who has been helpful, the library staff who has helped find books for your projects.)

 ## Treat

Dip

Mix together:
8 ounce package cream cheese
3 Tbs. creamy peanut butter
2 Tbs. bacon bits
Enough milk to make the mixture soft enough to use
as a vegetable dip (start with 1 tablespoon).

 ## Poem

Anonymous. "Mr. Finney's Turnip." In *A Child's Book of Poems,* by Gyo Fujikawa. Grosset & Dunlap, 1974.

 ## Word Play

A carrot top sometimes is used to refer to a person with red hair.
When you want to know what is causing a problem, you say, "I want to get at the root of this."
If someone is embarrassed, they may turn beet red.
And here is a root vegetable joke:
Band Student #1: What was John Philip Sousa's vegetable?
Band Student #2: The beet.

Read More About It

Florian, Douglas. *Vegetable Garden.* Harcourt Brace Jovanovich, 1991. 32 pp. (P).

Kite, L. Patricia. *Gardening Wizardry for Kids.* Barron's, 1995. pp. 2-69. (P-I).

Krauss, Ruth. *The Carrot Seed.* HarperCollins, 1945. 25 pp. (P).

Pellowski, Anne. "Why Carrots Are the Color of Flame." In *Hidden Stories in Plants.* Macmillan, 1990. p. 8. (I).

Selsam, Millicent. *The Carrot and Other Root Vegetables.* Morrow, 1971. 48 pp. (P-I).

Tolstoy, Alexei. *The Great Big Enormous Turnip.* Watts, 1968. 34 pp. (P).

Wolf, Janet. *The Rosy Fat Magenta Radish.* Little, Brown, 1990. 32 pp. (P).

4.2 Salad Gardens

Johnson, Hannah L. *From Seed to Salad.* Lothrop, Lee & Shepard, 1978. 48 pp. (I).

Planning, digging, planting, watering, weeding, harvesting—all the steps necessary for growing salad fixin's are shown. Black-and-white photographs portray the progress made by a group of boys and girls as they "grow a salad." Included are recipes for salad dressing and even an onion/garlic formula to spray on vegetable plants to keep the insects at bay.

Gardening Activity

Salad Gardens

Have your boys and girls plant a salad garden in your group's garden plot or in large containers such as planters or half-barrels, or you might try filling a large trash bag with garden soil that has been amended with compost: Tie the open end shut, then lay the trash bag planter where it will receive six hours of sunlight. Have the children plant looseleaf varieties of lettuce such as oakleaf, simpson, or red sails because these will mature in about 45 days. They may also like to grow cucumbers; bush varieties grow well in pots and mature in less than 60 days. Radishes flavor a salad and are easily grown in containers.

Language Arts Activity

Mixed-Up Word Game

A salad is a mixed-up mess of vegetables. Following is a set of salad words that are all mixed up. Place these words on paper, chalkboard, or an overhead transparency and have the children unscramble them. You may want to time them. You may want to have them work individually or in partners or teams.

Mixed-up words:

1. asrihd	4. vhecis	7. vneedi
2. etutelc	5. elyerc	8. gbeaacb
3. mottao	6. ermnoia	9. srtaorc

Answers:

1. radish	4. chives	7. endive
2. lettuce	5. celery	8. cabbage
3. tomato	6. romaine	9. carrots

Creative Activity

Seed Packet Collages

A salad may be a mix of many different fruits, vegetables, and nuts. A collage in the art world is a mix of many textures, media, and colors. Often the artist has a theme that unites the various pieces. Have your boys and girls make seed packet collages. For each child, have on hand a dozen or so seed packets with pictures, seed catalogs, seeds, white glue, dried plant material, and tagboard (used file folders make a good recycled substitute).

Have the boys and girls experiment with arrangements before they glue them to the tagboard. These collages would make an attractive bulletin board background for a display of garden-related books at a local public or school library, a display of garden-related crafts at the county fair, or a store-window display of vegetables and flowers grown by your group.

Treat

> ### Salad Bar
>
> Have on hand a variety of lettuce, tomatoes, cucumbers, and radishes harvested from your group's garden plot or container gardens. Boys and girls may pick and choose ingredients for their salads. You may wish to make Tasha Tudor's French Dressing from the *Tasha Tudor Cookbook* (Little, Brown, 1993) or this one, which has a Puerto Rican flavor:
>
> 1/2 cup olive oil   1 tsp. salt
> 2 Tbs. lemon juice   1/2 tsp. ground black pepper
> 1 garlic clove, minced   2 Tbs. chopped olives
> 1 Tbs. catsup   1/4 tsp. sugar
>
> Pour all the ingredients into a jar with a lid. Shake hard until creamy.

Poem

Steele, Mary Q. "Lettuce." In *Anna's Garden Songs*. Greenwillow, 1989.

Word Play

When people are young and successful, they are living in their salad days.
People with a lot of paper money have a lot of lettuce or cabbage in their wallets.

Read More About It

Brown, Marc. "Grow a Salad." In *Your First Garden Book*. Little, Brown, 1981. 48 pp. (P).

Daddona, Mark. *Hoe, Hoe, Hoe. Watch My Garden Grow.* Addison-Wesley, 1980. 58 pp. (P).

Lottridge, Celia Barker. *One Watermelon Seed.* Oxford University Press, 1986. 24 pp. (P).

Lovejoy, Sharon. "A Garden of Greens." In *Sunflower Houses.* Interweave, 1991. pp. 48-49. (I).

Tilgner, Linda. "Grow a Mixed Salad Bed." In *Let's Grow!* Storey Communications, 1988. pp. 52-54. (I).

4.3 Easy and Early Vegetables

Walters, Jennie. *Gardening with Peter Rabbit.* Warne, 1992. 46 pp. (P-I). Illustrations.

Divided by the seasons, the text provides directions for 20 garden-related projects. An "easy and early" project may be found on page 18. Beatrix Potter illustrations decorate every page.

Gardening Activity

Early Vegetable Gardens

Have your boys and girls plant vegetable varieties that can be harvested shortly after planting. These include radishes (22 days), patty pan squash (50 days), spinach (40 days), and carrots (55 days). Also to be tried is a bush bean such as Gold Crop wax or yellow wax beans that are ready for harvest in 45 days. Be sure the boys and girls check the days-to-harvest information given in the seed catalogs or on the seed packets as they make their choices.

Language Arts Activity

Connect the Syllable Silly Sentences

Using vegetable and vegetable-related names as the first word, have your children make up silly sentences by making the next word in the sentence begin with the last syllable of the previous word. Have dictionaries on hand. For example:

Radish dishes escape Capetown towncrier.

For younger children, use the last letter of the previous word to begin the next word in the sentence. For one-syllable words such as *corn,* use the phonogram -orn. These words will work: *garden, vegetable, radish, spinach, pumpkin, carrot, asparagus,* and *cabbage. Lettuce* is almost impossible. Have fun.

Creative Activity

Vegie Lotto

Have on hand these materials: gardening magazines and seed catalogs, glue, scissors, dried lima beans for markers, and 8½" x 11" tagboard cards divided into 30 squares in the style of a lotto or bingo card.

Write the letters V-E-G-I-E in the top five spaces. Distinguish the two *Es* from each other by making them different colors or sizes. Have the boys and girls cut out vegetable and gardening pictures from the magazines and seed catalogs. Have them paste one picture in each square in a random fashion. Remind them not to repeat any picture on the same card. After the cards are completed, make a master list of all the words represented among the cards. Call out the words in random order. Remember to distinguish the two *Es* by color or size when you call them out.

Treat

Oakleaf Lettuce Salad

Oakleaf lettuce	1/2 cup yellow squash, diced
Green leaf lettuce	green onion, chopped
1/2 cup carrots, grated	2 Tbs. basil, minced

Wash and tear the lettuce. Place it into a bowl with the chopped vegetables. Toss. Pour on a favorite salad dressing.

(From *The Children's Garden Cookbook*. Brooklyn Botanic Gardens. Used with written permission.)

 Poem

Aldis, Dorathy. "Mister Carrot." In *All Together: A Child's Treasury of Verse*. Putnam's, 1959.

 Word Play

"Radishes!" is an expression of annoyance or disgust.

Read More About It

Graham, Ada, and Frank Graham. *Dooryard Garden*. Four Winds Press, 1974. pp. 29-35. (I).

Hershey, Rebecca. *Ready, Set, Grow!* Goodyear, 1995. 104 pp. (P-I).

Hunt, Linda, Marianne Frase, and Doris Liebert. *Celebrate the Seasons*. Herald Press, 1983. 163 pp. (P-I).

Kite, L. Patricia. *Gardening Wizardry for Kids*. Barron's, 1995. 220 pp. (P-I).

Paul, Aileen. *Kids Outdoor Gardening*. Doubleday, 1978. 77 pp. (I).

Rapp, Joel. *Let's Get Growing*. Prince Paperbacks, 1993. 96 pp. (I).

4.4 Mini-Vegetables

Lovejoy, Sharon. *Sunflower Houses.* Interweave, 1991. 144 pp. (I).

Although it is the quintessential book for constructing hideaways, *Sunflower Houses* is the only book in this collection that refers to growing miniature vegetables. Interspersed throughout the poems, quotations, fun activities, and flower lore are encouragements to grow mini-vegetables. On pages 46 and 47 Lovejoy describes the mini-trough she created for tots. Miniature vegetable varieties are listed.

Gardening Activity

Mini-Vegie Garden

Grow a garden of miniature vegetables. This chart suggests names and sources.

Vegetable	Variety	Source
Beets	Baby Gladiator	Gurney's
Carrots	Thumbelina	Park
Corn	Mini Blue	Gurney's
Eggplant	Bambino	Burpee
Pumpkins	Baby Boo	Park
Pumpkins	Munchkins	Harris
Squash	Peter Pan	Harris
Sweet pepper	Jingle Bells	Shepherds
Tomato	Sweet Million	Park
Watermelon	Sugar Baby	Harris
Zucchini	Roly Poly	Burpee

Language Arts Activity

Mini-Books

Following the pattern given in figure 4.1, have your boys and girls fold and cut 8½" x11" paper as directed to make blank mini-books. Have them write vegetable-related jokes and riddles. Sources can be found in *Tomatoes and Other Killer Vegetable Jokes and Riddle* (Doherty, 1992) by Stephanie Johnson.

Creative Activity

Mini-Magnets

Have on hand these materials: a batch of craft dough, magnet strips, tempera paint, paintbrushes, and white glue.

To make craft dough: Mix 4 cups flour, 1½ cups warm water, and 1 cup salt together. Knead for five minutes on a floured board. Refrigerate the part not being used. Have the children form vegetable shapes. After the items have been formed, bake for an hour at 325° F. Paint as appropriate. Glue a magnet on each.

Treat

Stuffed Roly Poly Zucchini

6 Roly Poly zucchinis   2 tsp. chopped green onions
8-ounce package   1 Tbs. milk
    cream cheese   1/2 cup corn cooked with 2 Tbs.
dash of paprika   diced green pepper
salt and pepper   1 tsp. minced parsley

Parboil the zucchini for 10 minutes. Scoop out the centers and chop. Mix chopped zucchini with the remainder of the ingredients. Fill zucchini shells. Place in a greased baking pan. Cover bottom with water. Bake at 350° for 20 minutes.

Poem

Field, Rachel. "Vegetables." In *A Small Child's Book of Verse*, by Pelagie Doane. Oxford University Press, 1948.

Read More About It

Ehlert, Lois. *Growing Vegetable Soup.* Harcourt Brace Jovanovich, 1987. 32 pp. (P).

Florian, Douglas. *Vegetable Garden.* Harcourt Brace Jovanovich, 1991. 32 pp. (P).

Kuhn, Dwight. *More Than Just a Vegetable Garden.* Silver Burdett, 1990. 40 pp. (P-I).

Porter, Wes. *The Garden Book.* Workman, 1989. 64 pp. (I).

Rhoades, Diane. *Garden Crafts for Kids.* Sterling/Lark, 1995. 144 pp. (I).

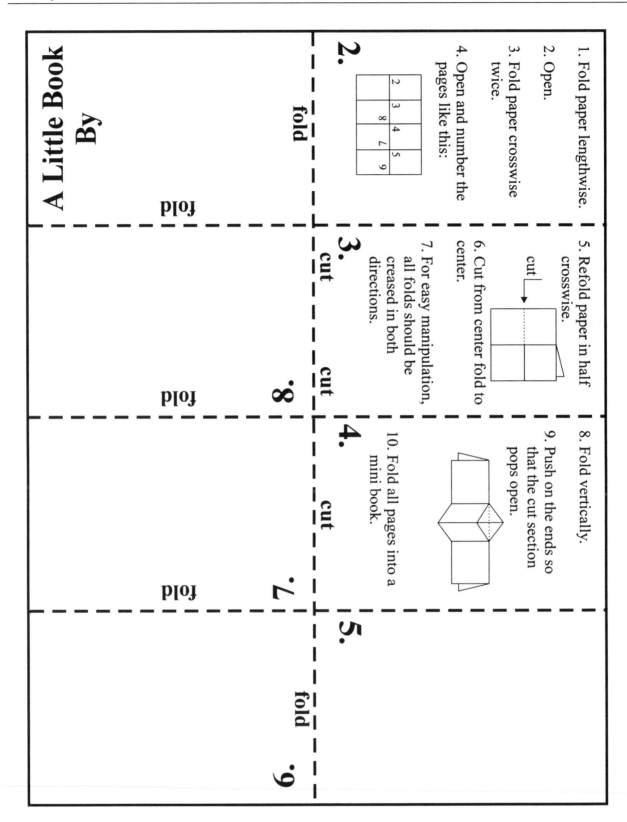

Fig 4.1. Mini-book pattern

From *Cultivating a Child's Imagination Through Gardening.* © 1996. Nancy Allen Jurenka and Rosanne J. Blass. Teacher Ideas Press. (800) 237-6124.

4.5 Giant Vegetables

Stevenson, James. *Grandpa's Too-Good Garden.* Greenwillow, 1989. 32 pp. (P).

Grandpa tells Louie and Mary Ann what happened when his grandfather's hair tonic spilled out into the garden. For one thing, giant vegetables flourished. This humorous fantasy is a fine book to read aloud to your group. James Stevenson's droll cartoons will please readers.

Gardening Activity

Giant Vegetable Contest

Over the growing season, have a contest among the members of your group to see who can grow the largest vegetable in several varieties. Cabbages, pumpkins, corn, cucumbers, zucchini, and squash are some to try. In Derek Fell's book, *A Kid's First Book of Gardening,* are several suggestions for giant vegetables. Peruse seed catalogs for ideas. Giant varieties sometimes appear in the novelty section of the catalog and sometimes under each vegetable. It is important that the children order the correct type of seed for giant vegetables.

Language Arts Activity

Tall Tales

Grandpa, fishermen, and gardeners love to tell whoppers or tall tales. Read a selection of American tall tales to your group. Then have your children concoct tall tales about one of their giant plants. Construct a large book (18" x 36") by binding newsprint with a poster board cover. Have your boys and girls copy their tall tales into the big book.

Creative Activity

Giant Vegetable Quilt

Have on hand these materials: rolls of colored bulletin board paper, wallpaper sample books, magazines, scissors, crayons, markers, glue, and 12" x 18" manilla drawing paper.

Assign each child a vegetable to draw and decorate in a fanciful way. Give each child a piece of manilla drawing paper. Have them draw the outline of a vegetable; encourage them to fill up as much of the paper as possible. Then have them fill in the outline of the vegetable using smaller designs with crayons and markers or torn pieces of wallpaper and magazine pictures.

Glue their fanciful giant vegetables within rectangles marked off on a long piece of bulletin board paper, say 36" x 126". Hang the giant vegetable "quilt" on a tall wall.

Treat

> # Giant Zucchini Cookies
>
> 3/4 cup shortening   2 scant cups flour
> 3/4 cup sugar   2 tsp. baking powder
> 1/2 tsp. salt   1 cup grated zucchini
> 1 Tbs. orange zest   1/2 cup chopped pecans
> 1 egg beaten with 2 Tbs. water
>
> Blend shortening and sugar. Add egg, water, and zucchini. Sift together the dry ingredients, and stir them into the mixture. Stir in the chopped pecans and the orange zest. Drop by tablespoon onto a greased cookie sheet. Bake at 375° F for 12 to 15 minutes.
>
> Optional: Frost with a butter and confectioners' sugar icing flavored with 1 tablespoon each orange peel and orange juice.

Poem

Antin, Esther. "The Garden." In *Rainbow in the Sky,* by Louis Untermeyer. Harcourt Brace, 1963.

Read More About It

dePaola, Tomie. *Jamie O'Rourke and the Big Potato.* Putnam, 1992. 32 pp. (P).

Fell, Derek. *A Kid's First Book of Gardening.* Running Press, 1989. 96 pp. (I).

Kroll, Steven. *The Biggest Pumpkin Ever.* Scholastic, 1984. 32 pp. (P).

Siracusa, Catherine. *The Giant Zucchini.* Hyperion, 1993. 45 pp. (P).

Westcott, Nadine B. *The Giant Vegetable Garden.* Atlantic Monthly, 1981. 32 pp. (P).

Chapter 5
NATURE'S GARDENS

This chapter introduces children to books and activities related to ecology, organic garden-ing, and interdependence between plants, animals, and humans. Ecosystems and biomes are described and explored. Activities focus on living in harmony with our environment, exploring environmental interrelationships, collecting specimens and plants, and creating dioramas and mini-ecosystems. Opportunities for community outreach include preparing a community photo exhibit, inviting a County Extension agent to meet with your boys and girls, and exploring an outdoor area such as a playground, meadow, empty lot, or lawn in your community. Finally, boys and girls will have an opportunity to enrich their human habitat by selecting books, music, and games to take with them as members of a simulated Biosphere 2 team.

5.1 Ecology

Durell, Ann, Jean Craighead George, and Katherine Paterson (eds.). *The Big Book for Our Planet.* Dutton, 1993. 136 pp. (I).

Award-winning authors and illustrators of books for children and young adults contributed to this collection of stories, essays, poems, limericks, photos, drawings, and cartoons designed to encourage readers to live in harmony with their environment. A list of organizations to which the reader can write for more information is given at the end. Their addresses and a brief description of their purposes are included. In some libraries this book is cataloged under "Aliki" because she is listed first alphabetically under the numerous authors. Reading and classroom teachers accustomed to a specific definition of "big book" may be surprised that the book is a regular size.

Gardening Activity

Your Choice

Select an activity of your choice that represents living in harmony with your environment to incorporate in your gardening projects. You may want to try companion planting, organic gardening, or water conservation. Discuss and select an activity appropriate to your community and gardening needs.

Language Arts Activity

Read and Respond

Read aloud and reenact Pam Conrad's "The Earth Game" or read and respond to Jim Arnosky's "Letter from Crinkleroot." Older boys and girls may want to research the history and origin of parks in their own communities after reading Milton Meltzer's "People's Gardens: Frederick Law Olmstead and the First Public Parks." These selections are found in *The Big Book for Our Planet.*

Creative Activity

Community Photo Exhibit

Take photos in your community and prepare an exhibit titled "Living in Harmony with Our Environment." Have your children take photos that stress human interaction with nature. Contact your public library, community center, or senior center about hosting the exhibit. If you like, you can extend this activity by having the children promote the exhibit (e.g., write and distribute press releases and typeset flyers and invitations).

Treat

┌───┐
| |
| ## Onion Soup with Garlic Toast |
| |
| Serve onion soup with garlic toast. |
| |
| |
| |
└───┘

Poem

Wadsworth, Olive A. *Over in the Meadow.* Puffin Books, 1985.

Word Play

Enjoy the limericks and cartoons in *The Big Book for Our Planet.*

Read More About It

Cochrane, Jennifer. *Plant Ecology.* Bookwright Press, 1987. 47 pp. (I).

Elkington, John, Julia Hailes, Douglas Hill, and Joel Makowee. *Going Green.* Puffin, 1990. 112 pp. (I).

Newton, James R. *A Forest Is Reborn.* Crowell, 1982. 28 pp. (P-I).

Patent, Dorothy Hinshaw. *Yellowstone Fires.* Holiday House, 1990. 40 pp. (I).

Van Allsburg, Chris. *Just a Dream.* Houghton Mifflin, 1990. 48 pp. (P-I).

5.2 Organic Gardening

Readman, Jo. *Muck and Magic*. Search Press, 1993. 48 pp. (P-I). Illustrations by Polly Pinder.

A British garden writer and mother of two young boys, Readman has written an organic gardening book for children. It covers the basics of gardening, soil improvement, plant propagation, pest control, and the cultivation of fruits, vegetables, and flowers. It is an activity-oriented book with something to do on each page. Conservation of and respect for the environment are emphasized. A gardening board game adds to the fun.

Gardening Activity

Companion Planting

Use companion planting as a natural deterrent to garden pests. Try a combination of leaf lettuce, tomato plants, sweet alyssum, and French marigolds. Intersperse onion and garlic sets throughout your garden. Research and try other combinations. The book *Carrots Love Tomatoes* (Storey Communications, 1976) by Louise Riotte will get you off to a good start.

Language Arts Activity

County Extension Service

Telephone or write to your County Extension Service for free literature and information about organic gardening. Be sure to ask for the names of insect- and disease-free plants appropriate to your area. You may wish to invite a County Extension agent to meet with your boys and girls. Be sure to discuss and generate a list of questions in preparation for the meeting.

Creative Activity

Garden Calendar

Develop a garden calendar appropriate to your area.

Treat

Organic Fruits and Vegetables

Serve a tray of organically raised fruits and vegetables.

Poem

Vipont, Elfrida. "For All the Joys of Harvest." In *Shoots of Green,* by Anne Harvey. Greenwillow, 1991.

Read More About It

Davis, Brenda. *Newer and Better Organic Gardening.* Putnam, 1976. 95 pp. (I).

Fenten, D. X. *Gardening Naturally.* Watts, 1973. 87 pp. (I).

Fryer, Lee, and Leigh Bradford. *A Child's Organic Garden.* Acropolis, 1989. 96 pp. (I).

Gay, Kathlyn. *Cleaning Nature Naturally.* Walker, 1991. 137 pp. (I).

Kohn, Bernice. *The Organic Living Book.* Viking, 1972. 72 pp. (I).

Mintz, Lorelie M. *Vegetables in Patches and Pots.* Farrar, Straus & Giroux, 1976. 116 pp. (I).

5.3 Interdependence

Norsgaard, E. Jaediker. *Nature's Great Balancing Act: In Our Own Backyard.*
Cobblehill, 1990. 64 pp. (I). Photographs by Campbell Norsgaard.

The Norsgaards take us on a walk around their backyard, which they have allowed
to grow wild. They point out the interdependence that exists among humans, plants,
mammals, birds, and insects. They also explain what people have done to throw
natural life out of balance and how we can restore it.

Gardening Activity

Outdoor Exploration

Select an outdoor environment in which to explore the interrelationships of plants, animals,
insects, and birds. Collect items to use in your shoe box diorama.

Language Arts Activity

Choral Reading and Poetry Writing

Use "The Tree in the Wood" by Duncan Enrick for choral reading. Then have your group
use it as a model to write their own cumulative poem.

Creative Activity

Shoebox Diorama

Create a shoebox diorama of the interrelationships you discovered in your outdoor explorations.

Treat

Interdependent Vegies

carrot sticks
celery sticks
vegetable dip

Serve carrots and celery in a simple display of interdependence.
Cut the vegetables into relatively equal lengths and divide into
groups of three. Set each group up tipi fashion, with the three
vegies leaning together. When one is taken away, the structure
falls down. You may need to dab the bottom ends in dip to keep
them in place on your serving tray.

Poem

"The Tree in the Wood." In *American Folk Poetry: An Anthology,* ed. Duncan Enrick. Little, Brown, 1974.

Read More About It

Hirschi, Ron. *Saving Our Prairies and Grasslands.* Delacorte, 1994. 65 pp. (I). Photographs by Erwin and Peggy Bauer.

Kuhn, Dwight. *More Than Just a Vegetable Garden.* Silver Burdett, 1990. 40 pp. (P-I).

Pringle, Laurence. *Saving Our Wildlife.* Enslow, 1990. 64 pp. (I).

Wilkes, Angela. *My First Green Book.* Random House, 1991. 48 pp. (P).

Yolen, Jane. *Welcome to the Green House.* Putnam, 1993. 32 pp. (P-I). Illustrated by Laura Regan.

5.4 Nature Study

Morgan, Mary. *Benjamin's Bugs*. Bradbury, 1994. 44 pp. (P).

This book is a nature study primer. When Benjamin Porcupine and his mama take a walk, Benjamin stops to talk to an ant, taste a dandelion, climb a tree, turn over rocks, and watch crickets and earthworms. When Benjamin slips into the pond while trying to grab a fish, Mama comes to the rescue. She takes him home, gives him a hot bath, feeds him a snack, and puts him to bed. Children will identify with Benjamin and may be inspired to make their own nature discoveries.

Gardening Activity

Exploration

Explore an outdoor area. This could be a playground, a meadow, an empty lot, a park, a woods, or a tree lawn (those strips of grass and trees running parallel to a street). Pair the boys and girls or group by three. Have each group of children look for and select five natural items: the largest, the smallest, the most colorful, the most interesting shape, and the most unusual.

Language Arts Activity

Discuss and Summarize

Discuss the sets of five items each group of children selected during their outdoor explorations. Identify and describe the items and where they were found. Explain why they were selected. Have boys and girls write summaries of the discussion.

Creative Activity

Freely Box

Place items that children gathered during their outdoor explorations into a shoebox. In the lid, cut a hole just large enough for a child's hand. Tape the lid onto the box. Let each child feel and identify one item.

Treat

Grasshopper Sundaes

Serve grasshopper sundaes made with vanilla ice cream, mint, and chocolate toppings.

Poem

Keats, John. "The Grasshopper and the Cricket." In *Every Child's Book of Verse*, ed. Sarah Chokla Grass. Watts, 1968.

 ## Word Play

"Knee-high to a grasshopper" is a well-known idiom, as are "ants in his pants" and "fly in the ointment."

Read More About It

Baptista, Lynn Hardie. *Discover Rain Forests.* Forest House, 1992. 44 pp. (P-I).

Burnie, David. *How Nature Works.* Reader's Digest Association, 1991. 192 pp. (I).

Gove, Doris. *One Rainy Night.* Atheneum, 1994. unp. (I).

Hunken, Jorie. *Botany for All Ages.* Globe Pequot, 1993. 184 pp. (I).

Mitchell, Andrew. *The Young Naturalist.* Usborne House, 1989. 32 pp. (I).

Shanberg, Karen, and Stan Tekula. *Plantworks.* Adventure Publications, 1991. 159 pp. (I).

5.5 Ecosystems and Biomes

Gentry, Linnea, and Karen Liptak. *The Glass Ark: The Story of Biosphere 2.* Viking, 1991. 94 pp. (I-Adult).

Tightly sealed glass arches located near Tucson in Arizona's Sonoran Desert enclose a miniature replica of Earth the size of three football fields. The desert, rainforest, savannah, marsh, and ocean plus human habitat, farm, artificial lung, and mechanical systems comprise the self-contained world of Biosphere 2 in which water, air, and food are recycled to sustain plant, animal, and human life. The building of Biosphere 2, the selection of a team of eight people to live inside for a two-year period, visions for the future, basic data, a glossary, and a bibliography make for fascinating reading and set the stage for thought-provoking inquiry.

Gardening Activity

Create a Mini-Ecosystem

Depending on the size of your group, either pair boys and girls or organize them into small groups using the cooperative learning model. Select an ecosystem of interest and investigate plant life and growing conditions. Select and grow plants representative of that ecosystem, or create a mini-ecosystem of your choice. See *Bottle Biology* (Kendal-Hunt, 1993) by Paul Williams for suggestions for making models.

Language Arts Activity

Biosphere 2 Library

The human habitat of Biosphere 2 includes a library of books and videotapes. Compile a list of titles that you would want included in the Biosphere 2 library if you were selected as a team member. Ask family, friends, and neighbors to suggest titles to add to your list.

Creative Activity

Biosphere 2 Recreation

Biosphere 2 team members relax by reading, watching videotapes, playing chess and musical instruments, and listening to music. How would you entertain yourself if you were a member of the Biosphere 2 team? What games or musical instruments would you play? What music would you listen to?

Treat

Biospherian Dessert

Serve fruit salad with orange sherbet, which is the dessert included in the Sunday dinner menu on page 67 of *The Glass Ark*.

 **Poem**

Jernigan, Gisele. *Sonoran Seasons: A Year in the Desert.* Harbinger, 1994.

Read More About It

Baptista, Lynn Hardie. *Discover Rain Forests.* Forest House, 1992. 44 pp. (P-I).

Imagine a Biosphere: The Miniature World of Biosphere 2. Biosphere Press, 1990. (I).

Jernigan, Gisele. *Sonoran Seasons.* Harbinger, 1994. unp. (P-I).

Siy, Alexandra. *Native Grasslands.* Dillon Press, 1991. 71 pp. (P-I).

Stone, Lynn M. *Wetlands.* Rourke Enterprises, 1989. 48 pp. (I).

Vogelgesang, Jennifer. *Discovering Deserts.* Forest House, 1992. 44 pp. (P-I).

Chapter 6
PLANTS AROUND
THE WORLD

The garden is filled with geography, history, economics, marketing, global education, and political science lessons. This chapter highlights the reciprocal contributions made between the New World and Europe, the improvements that have turned plants into a multimillion-dollar business, the influences that plants have had on history, and the contributions made to our food supply by Native Americans.

6.1 Geographic Origins

Fenton, Carroll Lane, and Herminie B. Kitchen. *Plants We Live On.* John Day, 1971. 128 pp. (I).

The story, history, politics, geography, and families of food plants are described in this book. Especially well covered is the topic of foods contributed to our culture by Native American gardeners. The chapter on small grains traces the Middle Eastern origins of wheat and barley.

A detailed explanation of the organization of plants into families precedes a series of chapters that describe in fascinating detail the food plant members of various plant families. Genetics, plant improvement, a history of agriculture, and the problems associated with feeding a large world population conclude the book.

Gardening Activity

Sprout Wheat Seeds

Rinse wheat seeds, then soak them for 12 hours in warm water. Sprinkle a tablespoon of wheat seeds on wet cotton in a bowl. Cover the bowl with plastic and place it in a warm, dark place. Check daily.

When the seeds sprout, remove the plastic. Move them into the light. Spray with water daily. Snip sprouts and sprinkle on salad.

Language Arts Activity

Supermarket Investigation

Make maps, graphs, and charts showing the geographic origins of foods available in the supermarket.

Creative Activity

Wheat Braids

An English custom believed to ensure a plentiful harvest for next year calls for braiding wheat from the last sheaf to be harvested.

Have on hand these materials: five long straws of wheat with ears (the seed head), thread, scissors, and ribbon.

Soak the straws until pliable. Tie five straws together just below the ears. Braid together. Tie the end and fold it back to make a loop. Decorate with ribbon and a bow.

Treat

Sprout Salad

Prepare and serve garden salad sprinkled with wheat seed sprouts.

 ## Word Play

Sprout may be used as a verb meaning "to grow" or as a noun meaning "new growth." Sometimes *sprout* is a word adults use when they refer to a little child.

Read More About It

Dowden, Anne Ophelia. *Poisons in Our Path.* HarperCollins, 1994. 61 pp. (I).

Gibbons, Gail. *Nature's Green Umbrella.* Morrow, 1994. 32 pp. (P-I).

Holmes, Anita. *Cactus.* Four Winds, 1982. 192 pp. (I).

Kite, L. Patricia. *Gardening Wizardry for Kids.* Barron's, 1995. pp. 2-69. (P-I).

Limburg, Peter. *What's in the Name of Flowers.* Coward, McCann & Geoghegan, 1974. 190 pp. (I).

Meltzer, Milton. *The Amazing Potato.* HarperCollins, 1992. 116 pp. (I).

Priceman, Marjorie. *How to Make an Apple Pie and See the World.* Knopf, 1994. 32 pp. (P).

Selsam, Millicent. *Peanut.* Morrow, 1969. 48 pp. (P-I).

6.2 Travel Routes

Johnson, Janice. *Rosamund*. Simon & Schuster, 1994. 32 pp. (P-I). Illustrated by Deborah Haeffle.

From the sheltered gardens of King Henry II came a beautiful new rose, Rosa Mundi. From century to century, this rose played a role—generation by generation—in the lives of people who marched off to the Crusades, dealt with the War of the Roses, sailed to Massachusetts, trooped across the Oregon Trail, and settled by the Willamette River. This beautifully illustrated book is sure to capture the interest of those who enjoy old roses, history, and genealogy.

Gardening Activity

Friendship Garden

Plan and plant a friendship garden. Select plants that are of special meaning to you or your family, plants that have traveled with you and your family as you have moved from one home to another, or those that were gift plants. Ask friends and neighbors to contribute seeds or cuttings for your friendship garden.

Language Arts Activity

Research and Write

Discuss, then research and write a short history of a plant of your choice. The plant may be a flower, fruit, herb, or vegetable. Does that plant have a special meaning to your family? Has that plant had an impact on your family's lifestyle? Trace the geographical migration of your plant. Why did it follow that particular movement around the world, across North America, or within the United States? Has that plant or its uses changed as it migrated? How has it changed?

Creative Activity

Timelines, Maps, and Dioramas

Develop timelines and maps that show plant travel routes and dioramas that depict the special meaning or impact of plants.

Treat

Spanish Rose Sherbet

1 pint rose petals (pesticide free)
2 1/4 cups sugar
6 oranges, juiced

Wash the rose petals. Use a mortar and pestle to pound them into a paste.

Gradually add 1/4 cup sugar. Dissolve 2 cups sugar in 4 cups boiling water. Stir into rose paste. Boil 10 minutes. Cool and add the juice of the oranges. Freeze and serve. Garnish with fresh rose petals.

Poem

Lindsay, Vachel. "In Praise of Johnny Appleseed." In *Johnny Appleseed and Other Poems.* Macmillan, 1967.

Word Play

The origin and history of rose names are fascinating. For instance, the Peace Rose was sent to the United States on the last plane to leave France prior to World War II. It was named the day that Berlin fell and at the close of World War II became an international symbol. Damask and other old-fashioned roses have long and interesting histories.

Read More About It

Handelsman, Judith F. *Gardens from Garbage.* Millbrook, 1993. 48 pp. (P-I).

Kite, L. Patricia. *Gardening Wizardry for Kids.* Barron's, 1995. pp. 1-69 (P-I).

Limburg, Peter. *What's in the Name of Flowers.* Coward, McCann & Geoghegan, 1974. 190 pp. (I).

McDonald, Lucile. *Garden Sass.* Nelson, 1971. 192 pp. (I).

Nottridge, Rhoda. *Sugar.* Carolrhoda, 1990. 32 pp. (P).

Sobol, Harriet. *A Book of Vegetables.* Dodd, Mead, 1984. 46 pp. (P-I).

6.3 New Arrivals

Rahn, Joan Elma. *Plants That Changed History*. Atheneum, 1982. 144 pp. (I).
Rahn describes the impact that cereals, spices, sugarcane, potatoes, and coal forests have had on history. She recounts in this informative book how plants have influenced people's lifestyles.

Gardening Activity

Community Plant History

Is there a plant such as wheat, cotton, citrus, or perhaps coal forests that affected the history and economy of your community? If possible, obtain and start a seedling of that plant. Research the jobs that plant created for your community.

Language Arts Activity

Think and Discuss

Think about the impact of the products listed above on the lifestyles of people in the United States. Do these items have the same impact today as they did in the past? In what way? Why or why not?

Think about the impact of one of the plants on your own family's history. Were any of your ancestors affected in any way by any of these plants? If not, do you have friends or neighbors whose families might have been affected? If so, in what way?

Creative Activity

Mock TV Special

Organize and report the information you have gathered by preparing a script and producing a mock TV special.

Treat

Tasting Party

Plan a tasting party and serve a variety of "new arrivals," such as potato chips, sugar cubes, and an assortment of cereals.

Poem

Popa, Vasko. "Potato." In *The Earth Is Painted Green,* ed. Barbara Brenner. Scholastic, 1994.

Word Play

"Sweet as sugar," "black as coal," and "cheeks like an apple" are common figures of speech.

Read More About It

Dodge, Bertha. *Plants That Changed the World.* Little, Brown, 1959. 183 pp. (I).

Nottridge, Rhoda. *Sugar.* Carolrhoda, 1989. 32 pp. (P).

Oppenheim, Joanne. *Floratorium.* Bantam, 1994. 48 pp. (P-I). Illustrated by S. D. Schindler.

Rahn, Joan Elma. *More Plants That Changed History.* Atheneum, 1985. 144 pp. (I).

Selsam, Millicent. *Cotton.* Morrow, 1983. 48 pp. (P-I). Photographs by Jerome Wexler.

Wilson, Charles M. *Green Treasures.* Macrae Smith, 1974. 184 pp. (I).

6.4 Endangered Plants

Halpern, Robert R. *Green Planet Rescue: Saving the Earth's Endangered Plants.* Watts, 1993. 64 pp. (I).

Colorful photos and readable text present an attractive format and a fascinating introduction to an array of interdependence and interrelationships of the natural environment. Topics include new plant discoveries, plant-based medicines, the role of animals as gardeners, and how and why plant life becomes endangered. This book poses the problem of plant endangerment and offers suggestions for solving it. It concludes with names and addresses of conservation organizations.

 ## Gardening Activity

Community Plants

Identify the endangered plants in your own community. What efforts are being made to protect and preserve those plants?

 ## Language Arts Activity

Letter Writing

Compile a list of conservation organizations. Write to them for information about preserving and protecting endangered plants.

 ## Creative Activity

Three Good Things

Have a discussion with your youngsters sparked by the topic, "Here's What I Would Do to Save Endangered Plants." Tell your boys and girls that their ideas should be extremely expensive, almost impossible to carry out, and as creative as they can possibly make them. Give them three minutes to think about the topic. Tell them to scribble down as many outrageous ideas as they can come up with. After three minutes, tell them to pick the best idea on their lists and, in turn, share their idea with the group. As soon as an idea has been presented, ask everyone in the group to think of three good things about each of the ideas and to tell the person who presented the idea those three good things.

The purpose of this discussion is to help children think divergently and creatively about a problem without worrying what others will think of their solutions. Be sure to encourage your group to think up nearly impossible solutions if some are too humdrum. You are likely to notice after a while that within every outrageous idea there is a kernel of a viable activity that could actually be carried out by the group or individual.

Treat

Gummy Dinosaurs

Serve some extinct creatures in candy form.

 Poem

"Finders-Keepers, Losers-Weepers." In *Earth Lines: Poems for the Green Age*, ed. Pat Moon. Greenwillow, 1991.

Read More About It

Facklam, Howard, and Margery Facklam. *Plants.* Enslow, 1990. 96 pp. (I).

Hogner, Dorothy Childs. *Endangered Plants.* Crowell, 1977. 83 pp. (I).

Holmes, Anita. *Cactus.* Four Winds, 1982. 192 pp. (I).

Landau, Elaine. *Endangered Plants.* Watts, 1992. 60 pp. (I).

Ricciuti, Edward R. *Plants in Danger.* Harper & Row, 1979. 96 pp. (I).

6.5 New World Contributions

Hays, Wilma, and R. Vernon Hays. *Foods the Indians Gave Us.* Ives Washburn, 1973. 113 pp. (I).

For the budding ethnobotanist, here is an oldie but goodie. After an introductory chapter giving a general history of the New World, with an emphasis on the Incas, the Hays describe individual foods cultivated by Native Americans, North and South. Separate chapters are devoted to history, horticultural descriptions, market value, lore, and cultivation of foods such as peanuts, corn, potatoes, tomatoes, pineapples, chocolate, peppers, maple syrup, pumpkins, and beans. The book ends with recipes of Indian cooking. Included are Bean Hole Beans, Peanut Soup, and Iroquois Leaf Bread.

Gardening Activity

New World Garden

Plant a New World garden using potatoes, tomatoes, peppers, pumpkins, beans, corn, and other plants of your choice.

Language Arts Activity

List and Log

Compile a list of foods that originated in the Western Hemisphere. For one week, keep a log of the foods you eat. From your log, identify foods that originated in the Western Hemisphere.

Creative Activity

Cornhusk Heart Wall Hanging

Have on hand these materials: a wire clothes hanger, dried cornhusks, rickrack, a needle, thread, glue, and an ornament for the center.

Bend and shape the clothes hanger into the shape of a heart with the hanger end at the top. Cut cornhusks into $\frac{1}{4}$"-$\frac{1}{2}$" x 9" strips. Place each strip of cornhusk onto the heart frame using a clove-hitch knot. Do this until the frame is covered. Tie a piece of rickrack around your ornament and tie it to the heart frame so that it fills the center of the heart.

Treat

Hot Chocolate

Serve hot chocolate or select and prepare a recipe from *Foods the Indians Gave Us.*

Poem

"The Corn Grows Up from the Navaho Indians." In *The Earth Is Painted Green,* ed. Barbara Brenner. Scholastic, 1994.

Word Play

Homophones are words that sound alike but have different meanings. *Maize* and *May's* and *chili* and *chilly* are homophones.

Read More About It

Aliki. *Corn Is Maize.* Harper, 1976. 34 pp. (P-I).

Caduto, Michael, and Joseph Bruchac. *Native American Gardening.* Fulcrum, 1996. 158 pp. (I-Adult).

Fenton, Carroll Lane, and Herminie B. Kitchen. *Plants We Live On.* John Day, 1971. 128 pp. (I).

Grimm, William C. *Indian Harvests.* McGraw-Hill, 1973. 127 pp. (I).

Wilbur, C. Keith. *Indian Handcrafts.* Globe Pequot, 1990. 144 pp. (I).

Wyler, Rose. *Science Fun with Peanuts and Popcorn.* Messner, 1986. 48 pp. (P-I).

Chapter 7
LEGENDARY PLANTS

The activities in this unit provide the opportunity to incorporate multicultural education into your gardening program. Plants featured in this unit are gourds, Indian paintbrush, roses, pomegranates, and peonies. The gourd story comes from the southern Appalachian region. Other gourd stories can be found in Haitian and African traditions. Almost every culture in the world has a gourd story.

Native Americans have many folktales and legends related to plants. The one featured here is the southwestern legend of the Indian paintbrush, as retold by Tomie dePaola. In the "Read More About It" section is listed a Cherokee tale about Indian peace pipes.

The legend of the rose has two traditions: one Italian featuring Paula as the heroine, and the other from medieval Europe featuring Elizabeth. The latter can be found in Ruth Sawyer's *The Way of the Storyteller.*

The mythology of Greece produced the beautiful *Persephone and the Pomegranate* retold and illustrated by Kris Waldherr. This book will encourage your group to study the seasons.

From *Tales of a Chinese Grandmother* comes the poignant love story of the poet and a peony princess. The Chinese have a tradition of writing poetry to honor a flower. The poems are read aloud at family gatherings.

As in the other chapters, most of these sections will need to be stretched out over a growing season. The rose unit may be done in winter by growing miniature roses under grow lights. The pomegranate comes into season in mid-August and can be purchased at supermarkets through October, so this unit may be done in a few days within that time frame.

7.1 Gourds

Hunter, C. W. *The Green Gourd: A North Carolina Folktale.* Putnam, 1992. 32 pp. (P).

An old superstition states that if you pick a gourd before it is ripe, it will "witch" you. An old woman picks a green gourd and places it on her mantle. It jumps from the mantle and bops her on the head. She runs away from the gourd. In her attempts to escape the gourd's attack, she runs to the panther's house and then the fox's. At each house the gourd attacks the animal, causing it to run along with the old woman. Finally, the whole entourage reaches a boy's house. The boy smashes the gourd. The old woman, grateful to all the animals and the boy for helping her, invites them all back to her house for biscuits and homemade butter. The old woman never picks a green gourd again.

Gardening Activity

Gourd Garden

Plant gourd seeds. There are two basic kinds of gourds: thin-shelled and hard-shelled. Thin-shelled gourds are the small ornamental variety. Hard-shelled gourds are of many types, including snake, bottle, bushel, and birdhouse. These lend themselves to craft projects.

Prepare a 5-foot square of gardening space. Dig up the soil and amend it with organic material such as composted manure, grass clippings, leaves, and fertilizer. Rake the soil to free it of stones and dirt clods. Plant the seeds of hard-shelled gourds in a circle 4 feet in diameter. Water and mulch to keep the seeds under control. Erect poles around the circle to form a tipi. Train the vines up the poles. Keep the gourd vines watered and fertilized.

As an alternative to the tipi, your group may wish to train gourd vines along a wattle fence, as Native Americans might have done. This method is described in *Indian Handcrafts* (Globe Pequot, 1990) by C. Keith Wilbur.

Timing of the gourd harvest is important. Wait until after the first frost and then pick them, making sure that $1\frac{1}{2}$ inches of stem remains attached to each gourd.

After washing each gourd in a mild disinfectant (two tablespoons of borax in a quart of water), spread the gourds out to dry in a cool location out of direct sunlight. Gourds may also be hung up on a rack to dry. Check for mold every now and again. Throw out any that are too moldy. Allow the gourds to dry for at least two weeks.

Good information about gourd culture and craft may be obtained from:

American Gourd Society
P.O. Box 274
Mt. Gilead, OH 43338

The society has a newsletter with information about gourd seed sources and cultivation.

Language Arts Activity

Growing a Poem

Have your boys and girls observe gourds, gourd vines, and decorated gourds. Have them examine gourds closely. Ask your group, "What comes to mind when you think of gourds? What experiences have you had with them?" As they are giving you answers, create a semantic map (a graphic display of words showing their connections).

Do this by placing a circle in the middle of a chart, chalkboard, or whiteboard. Write the word *gourd* in the circle. Ask your group to tell you words that come to mind when they think of gourds and their personal experiences growing them. Write these words on the board all around the circle as fast as you receive responses from the children. It may begin to look like this:

birdhouses   vines

GOURDS

need lots of fertilizer   hard-shelled

mask

Eventually, it will become obvious that some words fall into a category. Therefore, place related words into a category. Ask the group to give you a title for that category. Now that a category has been created, you will find more words to fit in it.

Continue. Have the group think of other words and create new categories. After a while, it will become apparent that some of the categories are related to one another in some manner: sequential, cause/effect, comparison/contrast, opposites. Draw lines between these related categories and label the relationships. Now you have a map of the boys' and girls' thinking about the characteristics, functions, attributes, and relationships of gourds and gourd cultivation.

From the semantic map select a few words such as *gourd, birdhouse, mask, vine, tendril.* Write these across the top of a piece of chart paper, a chalkboard, or a whiteboard.

Ask the boys and girls to come up with rhyming words for these or other gourd-related words. Once the lists have been generated, write these lines (or better ones) on the board:

Gourds on a leafy vine,

Gourds on a leafy vine.

These serve as a set of first lines for subsequent verses of the poem. Each verse will begin with these two repeated lines.

Now ask the children to think of other gourd-related lines. Write them on the board. After the group has come up with two lines in verse form, end with this refrain:

Gourds on a leafy vine,

Gourds on a leafy vine,

We're having fun growing our

Gourds on a leafy vine.

Next, write a second verse following the same pattern. Your verses may read something like this:

Gourds on a leafy vine,

Gourds on a leafy vine.

Soon you'll be a cozy home

Little wren can call her own.

Gourds on a leafy vine,

Gourds on a leafy vine.

We're having fun growing our

Gourds on a leafy vine.

Continue in this manner until you and your group are satisfied that you have written (grown) a gourd poem. Recopy it onto tagboard and display it in a public spot, perhaps the bulletin board in your media center hallway.

Creative Activity

Gourd Crafts

The object to be made from the dried gourd depends on the type of gourd. The large hard-shelled lagenarias make excellent containers, planters, and birdhouses (see *Profitable Gourd Crafting,* listed under "Read More About It").

To make a birdhouse, cut a round hole in the biggest section of a bottle or birdhouse gourd with a keyhole saw. The size of the hole depends upon the bird you wish to attract. Wrens prefer a 1" hole; bluebirds, $1\frac{1}{2}$ ". Shake out the seeds and carefully clean out the inside of the gourd. Gourd shells can be brittle and easily damaged.

Decorative objects can be made from dipper, snake, and smaller lagenaria gourds. By gluing tagboard legs and plastic eyes to appropriately shaped gourds, dinosaurs can be fashioned to create a prehistoric tableau that your students might name "Gourdassic Park."

Luffa gourds produce luffa sponges, which make welcome gifts and profitable fund-raisers.

Treat

Roasted Pumpkin Seeds

Gourds are inedible but make great containers for other treats. They belong to the same genus as pumpkins. Boys and girls might like to roast pumpkin seeds and serve them in gourd bowls.

Seeds from a large pumpkin

1 tsp. salt   2 Tbs. cooking oil

Wash the seeds well in a strainer. Spread them out on paper towels to dry. Mix them with the oil and salt in a bowl. Spread them on a cookie sheet. Roast in a 250° F oven for 1-1/2 hours.

Word Play

When we want to express surprise or disbelief about what someone has done, we sometimes say, "You're out of your gourd!"

Read More About It

Caduto, Michael, and Joseph Bruchac. *Native American Gardening.* Fulcrum, 1996. 158 pp. (I-Adult).

Carpenter, Frances. "The Golden Gourd." In *South American Wonder Tales.* Follett, 1969. pp. 64-70. (I).

Chase, Richard. "The Green Gourd." In *Grandfather Tales.* Houghton Mifflin, 1948. pp. 213-221. (I).

Courlander, Harold. "Uncle Bouqui and Godfather Malice." In *Uncle Bouqui of Haiti.* Morrow, 1942. pp. 55-67. (I).

Kite, L. Patricia. *Gardening Wizardry for Kids.* Barron's 1995. 197-98 pp. (P-I).

Lovejoy, Sharon. "Wash with a Squash." In *Hollyhock Days.* Interweave, 1994. pp. 72-73. (I)

Nichols Garden Nursery. *Profitable Gourd Crafting.* (I). (Available from Nichols Garden Nursery, 1190 South Pacific, Albany OR 97321.)

7.2 Indian Paintbrush

dePaola, Tomie. *The Legend of the Indian Paintbrush.* Putnam, 1988. 38 pp. (P).

Little Gopher longed to ride with the hunters and warriors of his tribe, but his dream-vision guided him toward using his artistic talents. He steadfastly honored his gift and searched for just the right colors to paint the sunset. One day he found brushes filled with these colors upon a hillside. He painted the sunset and left the brushes on the hillside. The next morning the place was covered with the orange, red, and yellow flowers known today as Indian paintbrush.

Gardening Activity

Wildflower Garden

Indian paintbrush is a reddish-orange wildflower. Its fringed petals give it a brushy appearance. Obtain seeds of the Indian paintbrush and plant them. They require lots of sunshine, not too much water, and soil that's not too rich. If Indian paintbrush seeds or plants are not available or appropriate for your growing conditions, search for alternatives, for example, sundrops, owl's clover, Indian blanket, or hummingbird mint. Easy-to-grow wildflowers include purple coneflower and black-eyed Susan.

Does your neighborhood have a spot that could use a wildflower garden? How about a roadside, an empty lot, a median strip? Beautify your area with wildflowers.

Sources for wildflowers and wildflower information include the following:

Shepherd's Garden Seeds
30 Irene Street
Torrington, CT 06790

Johnny's
Foss Hill Road
Albion, ME 04910

A High Country Garden
2902 Rufina Street
Santa Fe, NM 87505-2929

National Wildflower Research Center
4801 LaCrosse Boulevard
Austin, TX 78739

Language Arts Activity

Name That Plant

Have on hand pictures of flowers and vegetables cut from seed catalogs. Be certain that the names of the plants don't show. Distribute these pictures among your group. Say to your group, "Here are pictures of flowers and vegetables. Make up names for them that are more colorful, descriptive, silly, vivid, or functional than the ones they already have. Study the pictures for clues that would help you give the plant a new name. For example, could lily of the valley be called Lady Guinevere's Bells? Could corn be called gold computer keys? Could creeping phlox be called Baby Bear's Pillow?"

Allow plenty of time for the boys and girls to think. After the plants have been renamed, have the children write legends or pourquoi stories that explain how the plant got its name.

Save the stories either by displaying them on a bulletin board or by binding them into a group book that has been illustrated with the seed catalog pictures.

Creative Activity

Tempera Paintings

Little Gopher wanted to paint. Have on hand manilla paper or mural paper, tempera paint, brushes, and water pots. Have the boys and girls paint to their heart's content.

Treat

Paint Pot Pudding

Make a batch of vanilla pudding and divide it into individual servings. To each serving stir in a table-spoon of jam to color the pudding. For blue add blue-berry jam; for pink, strawberry; for green, mint jelly; for orange, orange marmalade. For yellow it would be just as easy to make a batch of lemon pudding.

Poem

Fuiterman, Arthur. "Indian Pipe and Moccasin Flower." In *Sung Under the Silver Umbrella*. Macmillan, 1956.

Word Play

Other plants with names derived from Native Americans are Indian blanket, Indian pipes, and moccasin flowers.

Read More About It

Bell, Corydon. "The Origin of Indian Pipes." In *John Rattling Gourd of Big Cove*. Macmillan, 1955. pp. 76-80. (I).

Cathon, Laura E., and Thusnelda Schmidt. *Perhaps and Perchance*. Abingdon, 1962. 260 pp. (I).

Crowell, Robert L. *The Lore and Legends of Flowers*. Putnam, 1982. 80 pp. (I). Illustrated by Anne Ophelia Dowden.

dePaola, Tomie. *The Legend of the Bluebonnet*. Putnam, 1983. 32 pp. (P).

————. *The Legend of the Poinsettia*. Putnam, 1994. 32 pp. (P).

Kite, L. Patricia. *Gardening Wizardry for Kids*. Barron's, 1995. pp. 2-69 (P-I).

Pellowski, Anne. *Hidden Stories in Plants*. Macmillan, 1990. 93 pp. (I).

7.3 Roses

Jagendorf, M. A. "The Miracle of the Rose." In *The Priceless Cats and Other Italian Folktales.* Vanguard, 1956. 158 pp. (I).

In this ancient Italian folktale, Countess Paula, is a woman full of a generous spirit, married to an overbearing, selfish man. She sees suffering and starvation happening to people who live near their castle. She gives away what bread she can secretly get out of the castle. Unfortunately, her husband finds out, becomes furious, and forbids her to give away their food. He locks up the food in storage rooms.

Countess Paula is a very religious person and she prays long and hard about this situation. One day she happens to try a door to the storage room and finds that it is unlocked. She takes bread from the shelves and places the loaves in her apron. As she walks down the hall, she encounters her husband, who demands to know what she is carrying. When she opens her apron, all he can see are beautiful yellow roses. She offers him one to put in his cap and then goes on her way. The roses turn back into bread, which she distributes among the poor.

Her husband goes walking into the town, where he is seen by the town fool who laughs and points at the count's cap. When the count touches his cap, he finds that the rose there has also turned to bread. He understands the significance of this miracle and joins his wife in her ministry to the poor.

Gardening Activity

Roses in Pots

Under plant lights such as a GrowLab™, in a well-lit window, or outside if it is warm, cultivate miniature roses in large pots. Some varieties to be considered are Dee Bennett, Rise 'n Shine, and Golden Halo.

Park, Wayside, and Jackson and Perkins are a few of the mail order houses that supply rose plants.

Park	Wayside	Jackson and Perkins
Cokesbury Road	1 Garden Lane	P.O. Box 1028
Greenwood, SC 29647-0001	Hodges, SC 29695-0001	Medford, OR 97501

Ask your local nursery if they would consider contributing miniature roses for your rose growing project. Your group may also wish to write the following for information about rose culture:

American Rose Society
P.O. Box 30000
Shreveport, LA 71130-0030

Language Arts Activity

Diamante

This form of poetry calls for the writer to adhere to this specific structure:

First line: One word, a noun (usually the topic of the poem)

Second line: Two words that are adjectives

Third line: Three words ending in -*ing*, participles

Fourth line: Four words that create a phrase

Fifth line: Three participles

Sixth line: Two adjectives

Seventh line: A noun that may be a synonym of the first line

Have your boys and girls observe rose bushes quietly and intensely so that they acquire a real sense of "roseness." Have them write diamante poems based on their observations. Have the poems recopied in their best handwriting (or typing) and spelling into a group book. Their poems may also be written on individual papers to be displayed on a bulletin board that backs a table on which potted rose bushes have been arranged.

Creative Activity

Money-Raiser

Brainstorm with your group to come up with various ways to raise money to assist the less fortunate. Carry out your plans. The following are suggestions:

Have a Bread and Roses Sale. Sell baked goods and plants raised by the children.

Construct yellow paper roses to sell.

Obtain fresh yellow roses from a wholesaler to sell as a money-raiser.

Make beads from roses and string into necklaces to sell. Directions can be found on pages 464-465 of Rodale's *Illustrated Encyclopedia of Herbs* (Rodale Press, 1987).

Make rose petal potpourri to sell.

Treat

> ## Rose Hip Tea
>
> Either purchase rose hip tea from the grocery store or make your own if the season is right. In the autumn have your youngsters gather rose hips from roses grown on pesticide-free roses; double check to be sure that the rose gardener did not use a systemic pesticide during the growing season. Roses from the Rugosa family are recommended. Have the children rub off the whiskers from the hips. Cut off the stems. Wash the hips and place in a pan with enough water to cover them. Heat the water to boiling, then reduce the heat, and simmer for 15 minutes. Strain the tea and serve with honey. Rose hips can also be dried and stored for later use.

 Poem

Field, Rachel. "The Little Rose Tree." In *A Small Child's Book of Verse,* by Pelagie Doane. Oxford University Press, 1948.

 Word Play

Several sayings are associated with roses, such as:
"Everything is coming up roses."
"Everything's rosy."

Read More About It

Abell, Elizabeth. *Flower Gardening.* Watts, 1969. pp. 40-49. (I).

Crowell, Robert L. *The Lore and Legends of Flowers.* Putnam, 1982. pp. 41-51. (I). Illustrated by Anne Ophelia Dowden.

dePaola, Tomie. *The Lady of Guadalupe.* Holiday House, 1980. 46 pp. (P-I).

Earle, Olive. *The Rose Family.* Morrow, 1970. 44 pp. (P-I).

Ichikawa, Satomi. *Nora's Roses.* Philomel, 1993. 32 pp. (P).

Johnson, Janice. *Rosamund.* Simon & Schuster, 1994. 32 pp. (P-I). Illustrated by Deborah Haeffle.

Rapp, Joel. *Let's Get Growing.* Prince Paperbacks, 1993. pp.75-77. (I).

Sawyer, Ruth. "The Legend of St. Elizabeth." In *The Way of the Storyteller.* Macmillan, 1968. pp. 307-315. (I).

Slepian, Jan. *Risk 'n Roses.* Philomel, 1990. 175 pp. (I).

7.4 Pomegranates

Waldherr, Kris. *Persephone and the Pomegranate*. Dial, 1993. 32 pp. (P-I).

In this retelling of the ancient Greek myth, Persephone is lured and then snatched away to the underworld by Pluto. Upon discovering that her daughter has been stolen from her, enraged Demeter causes winter to be prolonged.

She bargains with Pluto for her daughter. Because Persephone had eaten six pomegranate seeds, she may stay with her mother for only six months. So the earth has six months of weather for growing and harvesting of crops and six months of cold weather.

Gardening Activity

Growing Seasons

Seasons are important to gardeners; they dictate what gardeners may or may not do. Make a list of as many gardening "things to do" as your boys and girls can think of. Engage your group in a classification exercise. As a group or individually, have them categorize these gardening tasks under these headings:

Things Gardeners Do in the Winter

Things Gardeners Do in the Spring

Things Gardeners Do in the Summer

Things Gardeners Do in the Fall

Use these lists to accompany the murals made during the Creative Activity.

Find out the dates of the last and first days of frost for your area. Why are these dates important? They mark the beginning and the end of the season gardeners love the most—the growing season.

Be sure your group knows the official dates for the first day of spring, summer, fall, and winter.

Language Arts Activity

Readers' Theater

In readers' theater, the actors read their parts while another person keeps the drama moving along by reading the narrative. Read aloud the story to your group of boys and girls. Working with your group, write out speaking parts for Persephone, Demeter, Zeus, Pluto, Hectare, Helios, a few human beings, Spring, and Winter. Some can be taken from the books while others will need to be created by your group. Assign the roles and put on a simple readers' theater production.

Creative Activity

Four Seasons Murals

Have on hand four large pieces of mural paper and tempera paints. Waldherr's illustrations suggest ancient murals or huge paintings on walls. Using Waldherr's colors (ochre, burnt sienna, olive, gold, and amber), have your group paint four murals representative of the four seasons. Divide the large group into four smaller ones and have them work cooperatively to decide the subjects and backgrounds.

Treat

Mediterranean Pomegranate Dessert
Fresh pomegranates are usually in season from August to October. They consist primarily of seeds with a tangy, citrus-like flavor. These are used in Middle Eastern cooking as a substitute for lemons.

2 pomegranates	1/2 cup sugar
1 cup water	juice of 1 lime

1 Tbs. rose water (may be purchased at Oriental and Middle Eastern markets)

Cut the pomegranates in half. Remove the seeds, taking care to retain the ruby pulp. Discard the white membrane without squashing the seeds. Combine the sugar and water. Boil a few minutes. Cool the syrup. Add the lime juice and rose water to the sugar syrup. Pour the syrup over the pomegranate seeds. Refrigerate a few hours before serving.

Poem

Gilchrist, Marie Emilie. "A Wreath for Persephone." In *Anthology of Children's Literature,* ed. E. Johnson and C. E. Scott. Houghton Mifflin, 1933.

Word Play

Demeter is the archetypal enraged parent who fights established society when a child has been taken away by death, drugs, disease, divorce, etc. Grief over such losses has led parents to form national organizations. We see Demeter's spirit today in M.A.D.D. (Mothers Against Drunk Drivers) and M.A.V. (Mothers Against Violence).

Read More About It

Cole, Joanna. *Plants in Winter.* Crowell, 1973. 32 pp. (P-I).

D'Aulaire, Ingri, and Edgar P. Parin. *Book of Greek Myths.* Doubleday, 1962. pp. 58-63. (I).

Farmer, Penelope, and Graham McCallum. *The Story of Persephone.* Morrow, 1973. 48 pp. (I).

Gibbons, Gail. *Reasons for Seasons.* Holiday House, 1995. 32 pp. (P-I).

Kite, L. Patricia. *Gardening Wizardry for Kids.* Barron's, 1995. pp. 92-93 (P-I).

McDermott, Gerald. *Daughter of Earth.* Delacorte, 1984. 32 pp. (P-I).

Rylant, Cynthia. *This Year's Garden.* Aladdin, 1987. 32 pp. (P-I).

7.5 Peonies

Carpenter, Frances. "The Poet and the Peony Princess." In *Tales of a Chinese Grandmother*. Doubleday Doran, 1937. pp. 124-133. (I). Reissued as a paperback by Charles E. Tuttle, 1973.

At Grandmother Ling's party one of the guests tells the story of a poet who fell in love with a beautiful woman wearing a rosy pink dress. She was, in fact, a flower princess named Siang Yu, who would have been doomed to die if the poet hadn't dreamed of a way to save her. They married and had a son. Eventually, the princess died of old age. When the poet's time to die came, he told his son to watch for new sprouts growing up beside Princess Siang Yu's peony plant. So it came about that the two peony trees grew side by side in the garden.

Gardening Activity

Gathering Bouquets in the Spring and Planting Peonies in the Autumn

In the spring, prepare to have a flower-honoring party in the custom of the Chinese grandmother in the story. Have your group gather many bouquets of peonies and other May-blooming flowers so that your meeting room or classroom is very festive.

Peony planting is best done in autumn. Have your youngsters plant a rosy pink and a white peony bush or tree peony in the garden where your group meets or in the garden of someone who needs and wants them. Peonies like an enriched soil to which organic matter such as compost or aged manure and a handful of bonemeal has been added. The hole should be dug 2 feet wide by 2 feet deep in a sunny location. The eyes or buds of the plant should be planted no deeper than 2 inches below ground level.

Language Arts Activity

Flower Poetry Scroll Book

Grandmother Ling hosted a party every year when the peonies were blooming. To honor her flowers, she invited the guests to recite a poem or tell a story about various flowers. Have your boys and girls search the literature to find flower poetry or stories. Have them share their flower poems and stories at the Peony Party, as is done in the Chinese tradition.

Collect the poems and stories and bind them into a scroll book. This can be constructed from wrapping paper tubing (you will need two) and mural paper cut to size. Attach one end of the mural paper to one tube and the other end to the second tube with white glue. Have the children copy their poems and stories in their best handwriting onto the mural paper.

Creative Activity

Flower-Honoring Party

Have a Peony Party or honor a flower that's more prevalent in your part of the country with a party. Who would you invite? Is there a retirement home in your neighborhood so that your boys and girls could adopt a grandmother to invite? Have your group write invitations. When the guests arrive, make a point of having your children greet them in a respectful manner. Serve refreshments; jasmine tea and almond cookies would be appropriate. Have the boys and girls read their poems and stories to the guests.

Appoint a child to thank the guests for attending the flower honoring party and to explain its roots in Chinese culture.

Treat

Jasmine Tea

Serve jasmine tea and almond cookies.

 ## Poem

Aldis, Dorathy. "Names." In *Sprouts of Green: Poems for Young Gardeners,* by Ella Bramblett. Crowell, 1968.

Read More About It

Cathon, Laura E., and Thusnelda Schmidt. *Perhaps and Perchance.* Abingdon, 1962. 260 pp. (I).

Crowell, Robert L. *The Lore and Legends of Flowers.* Putnam, 1982. 80 pp. (I). Illustrated by Anne Ophelia Dowden.

Demi. *The Empty Pot.* Holt, 1990. 32 pp. (P).

Gary, Charles, and Carol Watson. *Flower Fables.* EPM Publishers, 1978. 54 pp. (I).

Murphy, Louise. *My Garden.* Scribner's, 1980. 160 pp. (P-I). Illustrated by Lisa Campbell Ernst.

Pallotta, Jerry. *The Flower Alphabet Book.* Charlesbridge, 1988. 32 pp. (P-I). Illustrated by Leslie Evans.

Chapter 8
FICTIONAL GARDENERS

The child and animal as gardener in several genres of children's literature are presented in this chapter. Beginning with "Classics," which feature the work of Beatrix Potter, the lessons continue with "Good Reads" that present realistic and historical fiction. By contrast, the next set of lessons consists of fantasy, such as *The Flowers Festival* and *June 29, 1999*. "Multicultural Tales from the Garden" provides readers the opportunity to experience many cultures within a gardening theme. The many variations of Jack and the Beanstalk tales end the chapter.

8.1 Classics

Potter, Beatrix. *The Complete Tales of Beatrix Potter.* Warne, 1989. 383 pp. (P).
    This edition includes the 23 original, unabridged Peter Rabbit books with original color and black-and-white illustrations. The books are arranged in the order in which they were first published. Boys and girls may also enjoy listening to the audio tape of *The Tale of Peter Rabbit,* narrated by Carol Burnett, which is available from Music for Little People, P.O. Box 516, Montpelier, VT 05601, 1-800-223-6357.

Gardening Activity

Planting Book-Based Gardens

    Plant Peter Rabbit's garden after reading *The Tale of Peter Rabbit.* Plant lupines after reading *Miss Rumphius* (Puffin, 1994) by Barbara Cooney. Plant pomegranate seeds after reading "The Origin of the Seasons" in *Classic Myths to Read Aloud* (Crown, 1992) by William F. Russell. Use *The Secret Garden Notebook: A First Gardening Book* (Godine, 1991) by Graham Rust as a planting guide after reading *The Secret Garden* (Dell, 1990) by Frances Hodgson Burnett.

Language Arts Activity

Read Aloud

    Read aloud "The Origin of the Seasons" in William F. Russell's *Classic Myths to Read Aloud.* Compare this version of the Greek myth with other versions. Extend the activity by comparing the Greek myth with Native American tales such as "How the Seasons Came" or "Origin of Death and the Seasons" in *Nihancan's Feast of Beaver: Animal Tales of the North American Indians* (Museum of New Mexico Press, 1990) by Edward Lavitt and Robert E. McDowell.

Creative Activity

Sandburg's Corn Fairy Puppets

    Read Carl Sandburg's "How to Tell Corn Fairies When You See Them" in his *Rootabaga Stories.* Follow the description to create corn fairy puppets.

Treat

Walking Salad, Pomegranate Seeds, or Bread

After planting Peter Rabbit's garden, serve a Walking Salad: Wash and dry spinach or lettuce leaves. Put 2 tablespoons of cole slaw on each leaf. Boys and girls love to walk around eating these. You may prefer to serve pomegranate seeds after reading aloud "The Origin of the Seasons" or to serve bread after reading *The Little Red Hen.*

Poem

"Froggie Went A-Courting." In *American Folk Poetry: An Anthology,* ed. Duncan Enrick. Little, Brown, 1974. 831 pp.

Read More About It

Burnett, Frances Hodgson. *The Secret Garden.* Dell, 1990. 287 pp. (I).

Galdone, Paul. *The Little Red Hen.* Houghton Mifflin, 1973. 44 pp. (P).

Potter, Beatrix. *Mr. Jeremy Fisher.* Warne, 1989. 59 pp. (P).

————. *The Tale of Peter Rabbit.* Penguin, 1989. 57 pp. (P).

————. *The Tale of Timmy Tiptoes.* Warne, 1989. 59 pp. (P).

Sandburg, Carl. "How to Tell Corn Fairies When You See Them." In *Rootabaga Stories.* Harcourt Brace Jovanovich, 1988. pp 169-76. (I).

Southgate, Vera. *The Little Red Hen.* Ladybird Books, 1987. 51 pp. (P).

8.2 Good Reads

Slepian, Jan. *Risk 'n Roses*. Philomel, 1990. 175 pp. (I).

In this post-World War II, multicultural, urban tale of three preteen girls, we are drawn into the lives of Jean, a malicious street gang leader; Skip, an 11-year-old aching to be accepted; and Angela, her mildly retarded sister. As the story unfolds, we hope that Skip will come to her senses before the impending tragedy, that Jean gets her just desserts, and that Angela will be all right. Pivotal to the story is Mr. Kaminsky, who grows lovely roses despite much emotional pain. A suspenseful, beautiful book, it will appeal to the reader who appreciates the insights that a well-written psychological suspense novel can provide.

Gardening Activity

Design

Use landscape design templates and graph paper to design a garden from the book of your choice.

Language Arts Activity

Literature Circles

Provide time, multiple copies of garden-related works of fiction, and opportunity for groups of four or five children to meet periodically to discuss a book they have all been reading. Facilitate the discussion by saying, "Talk about the book that you have been reading. Share with each other the ideas and story parts you liked." Take an interested, active listener's role. Do not be a questioning, brow-beating inquisitor seeking answers to comprehension questions.

Creative Activity

Diorama

Have on hand these materials: shoeboxes, paper scraps, most any broken item that is about to be thrown away, bits of wood, pipe cleaners, glue, and crayons.

Say to the youngsters: "Create a shoebox diorama of the garden you designed or a garden scene from one of the books you've been reading."

Treat

Garden Party

Plan, prepare, and serve garden party refreshments to accompany the book of your choice.

Poem

Yolen, Jane. *An Invitation to the Butterfly Ball: A Counting Rhyme.* Boyds Mills Press, 1991.

Read More About It

Cooney, Barbara. *Miss Rumphius.* Viking, 1982. 32 pp. (P-I).

Gardiner, John R. *Top Secret.* Little, Brown, 1985. 110 pp. (I).

Quattlebaum, Mary. *Jackson Jones and the Puddle of Thorns.* Delacorte, 1994. 113 pp. (I).

Thomas, Elizabeth. *Green Beans.* Carolrhoda, 1992. 32 pp. (P).

Turner, Ann. *Grasshopper Summer.* Macmillan, 1989. 176 pp. (I).

8.3 Fantasy Stories and Gardens

Beskow, Elsa. *The Flowers' Festival.* Floris Books, 1991. 32 pp. (I).

In this fantasy, the Midsummer Fairy places a drop of poppy juice in Lisa's eyes to make her invisible so that she can join the flowers at their Midsummer Party. Flowers, vegetables, weeds, and house plants gather to celebrate Midsummer Eve with the birds and the bees, the crickets and the frogs. Queen Rose entertains her guests with refreshments, storytelling, poetry, music, and dance.

Charming illustrations and lively text introduce readers to an array of plants, flowers, and garden inhabitants and stimulate responses such as creative drama, play production, puppetry, readers' theater, choral reading, poetry, music, dance, and art.

Gardening Activity

Explore and Gather

Have boys and girls explore the meadow, lake, and woods as well as neighborhood gardens and vacant lots for flowers and plant materials. Gather blossoms and leaves to make potpourri.

Language Arts Activity

Journal Writing

Write a journal of meadow, lake, woods, and garden explorations. Describe flowers, plants, and wildlife found in each place, including the date of exploration. Extend the activity by revisiting each place over a period of time and describing the new flowers, plants, and wildlife found. Finally, describe the transformations that occur in flowers, plants, and wildlife as the seasons change.

Creative Activity

Illustrate and Recreate the Festival

Using seed catalogs, have boys and girls cut out pictures of flowers, plants, and vegetables that appear in *The Flowers' Festival.* Illustrate and re-create the festival by making line drawings to expand and elaborate on the pictures. Construct a mural and retell the story by adding written text composed by the boys and girls. Using the book as a model, encourage boys and girls to compose poetry as well as prose.

Extend the activity by developing a creative drama performance. Enliven the performance by using disguises and musical instruments made from plant materials. Directions can be found in Anne Pellowski's *Hidden Stories in Plants* (Macmillan, 1990). Encourage boys and girls with an interest in dance to choreograph the performance. The overture from Mendelssohn's "Midsummer Night's Dream" can be used as background music, especially for the procession of guests arriving at the party.

Treat

Refreshments

Plan, prepare, and serve party refreshments. A possible menu might be:
Iced Herbal Tea
Strawberry and Rhubarb Compote with Honey
Carrot and Zucchini Bread

Poem

Riley, James Whitcomb. "The Pixy People." In *Joyful Poems for Children,* ed. Bobbs Merrill, 1960. 157 pp.

Read More About It

Beskow, Elsa. *Peter in Blueberry Land.* Floris Books, 1987. unp. (I).

Burnett, Frances Hodgson. *The Land of the Blue Flower.* Kramer, 1993. 45 pp. (I).

Carroll, Lewis. *Alice in Wonderland and Through the Looking Glass.* Messner, 1982. 253 pp. (I).

Lamb, Charles, and Mary Lamb. "Midsummer Night's Dream." In *Tales from Shakspeare.* Crowell, 1942. 360 pp. (I).

Van Allsburg, Chris. *The Garden of Abdul Gasazi.* Houghton Mifflin, 1979. 33 pp. (P-I).

8.4 Multicultural
Tales from the Garden

Johnston, Tony. *The Tale of Rabbit and Coyote*. Putnam, 1994. unp. (P). Illustrated by Tomie dePaola.

This Mexican folktale illustrated by Tomie de Paola is about a series of pranks that the trickster Rabbit plays on Coyote. Finally angered by the pranks, Coyote chases Rabbit up a ladder into the moon. Unable to follow Rabbit up the ladder, Coyote howls at the moon to this day. The role of trickster appears in stories across cultures. Use this story as an introduction to trickster tales.

Gardening Activity

Design

Select a country that interests you. Plan and design a garden appropriate to that country.

Language Arts Activity

Trickster Puppet Show Script

Using Janet Stevens's book, *Tops & Bottoms,* a trickster tale, write a script for a puppet show. The words of Bear, Hare, and a narrator will suffice. After the show has been rehearsed and the puppets made, present the puppet show to an outside audience, such as another club or class, a retirement home group, or the children at an after school storytime at the public library.

Creative Activity

Puppets

Make paperbag puppets of Bear, Hare, and Hare's family to accompany the script of *Tops & Bottoms,* used for the Language Arts Activity.

Treat

Milk Shakes

Chocolate and vanilla are products from Mexico. Serve chocolate and/or vanilla milk shakes.

Poem

Herrara Alvarez, Leticia. "Country Memory." In *This Same Sky: A Collection of Poems from Around the World,* by Naomi Shihab Nye. Four Winds, 1992.

Read More About It

Aardema, Verna. *The Vingananee and the Tree Toad.* Warne, 1983. 48 pp. (P).

Boden, Alice. *The Field of Buttercups.* Walck, 1974. 32 pp. (P).

Bordewich, Fergus M. *Peach Blossom Spring.* Green Tiger, 1994. 42 pp. (P-I). Illustrated by Yang-Yi.

Bryan, Ashley. "Why Frog and Snake Never Play Together." In *Beat the Story-Drum, Pum-Pum.* Atheneum, 1980. 70 pp. (I).

Demi. *The Empty Pot.* Holt, 1990. 32 pp. (P).

Stevens, Janet. *Tops & Bottoms.* Harcourt Brace Jovanovich, 1995. 34 pp. (P).

8.5 Jack and the Beanstalk Tales

Wildsmith, Brian, and Rebecca Wildsmith. *Jack and the Meanstalk*. Knopf, 1994. unp. (P-I).

An experiment gets out of hand in this zany tale of Professor Jack, who concocts a formula calculated to make plants grow faster. Applied to some bean seeds, it causes a "meanstalk" to grow. Up the meanstalk grows into outer space. A space monster starts to crawl down the stalk, but root-chewing animals save the day destroying the plant at its roots. Boys and girls of all ages are sure to recognize and enjoy this contemporary version of an old favorite.

Gardening Activity

Bean Seed Trials

Have your group plant bean seeds. Place some in a light, warm place and some in a light, cool place. Place some in a dark, warm place and some in a dark, cool place. Ask your boys and girls to record and compare growth of the seeds. As an alternative, you may wish to have a race to see which child can grow the tallest red runner-bean plants or be the first to reach a predesignated height.

Language Arts Activity

Read, Compare, and Write

Read aloud and compare "Jack" tales. Have your youngsters write a new variant.

Creative Activity

Creative Dramatics

Act out the Jack tale of your choice.

Treat

Beanstalk Salad

Mix together 6 cups of cooked or canned beans: kidney, green, lima, black, wax, and pinto. Add 1 small sliced onion and 1 chopped green pepper. Dress with 1/2 cup oil, 1/2 cup vinegar, and 3/4 cup sugar.

Poem

St. Vincent Millay, Edna. "The Bean Stalk." In *Edna St. Vincent Millay's Poems Selected for Young People*. Harper, 1951.

Word Play

"Spilled the beans" is a saying that means that someone has told a secret. In the business world, an accountant is sometimes referred to as a bean counter.

Read More About It

Briggs, Raymond. *Jim and the Beanstalk*. Coward-McCann, 1970. 40 pp. (P).

Chase, Richard. *The Jack Tales*. Houghton Mifflin, 1943. 201 pp. (I).

Garner, Alan. *Jack and the Beanstalk*. Doubleday, 1992. 32 pp. (P-I). Illustrated by Julek Heller.

Kellogg, Steven. *Jack and the Beanstalk*. Morrow, 1991. 48 pp. (P).

Still, James. *Jack and the Wonder Beans*. Putnam, 1977. (P-I).

Chapter 9
FAMOUS GARDENERS

Biographies are featured in this last chapter. Here are portrayed the lives of famous plant scientists, botanists, and gardeners. These books are most likely to appeal to older children. George Washington Carver, Johnny Appleseed, Beatrix Potter, Rachel Carson, and other plant and nature lovers such as Aldo Leopold, Edward Palmer, Charles Darwin, Frederick Olmsted, and Luther Burbank come to life through these books and activities.

Chart and list the products that George Washington Carver developed from peanuts and sweet potatoes. Make up your own tall tales about Johnny Appleseed. Make up your own secret code and use it for writing as Beatrix Potter did. Listen to and identify the sounds of nature as Rachel Carson did. And finally, research careers in forestry conservation, plant science, biology, and botany.

9.1 George Washington Carver

Aliki. *A Weed Is a Flower: The Life of George Washington Carver*. Prentice-Hall, 1965. 32 pp. (P).

Even as a youngster, George Washington Carver was called the "Plant Doctor" because he took such good care of his garden that the townspeople came to him with their gardening questions. From his small town, he went to the university where he became a plant scientist. Many of the results of his experiments are still put into practice today. His advice about sweet potato and peanut propagation resulted in successful cash crops for southern farmers.

Gardening Activity

Soil Improvement

Professor Carver taught his students how to improve the soil by composting, by planting nitrogen-rich crops such as cowpeas, and by practicing crop rotation. How do these practices enrich the soil? What do gardeners in your community do to improve the soil? Do you have a garden plot that would benefit from soil improvement? How might you enrich the soil in your plot? Read chapter 3, pages 25 through 33, in Diane Rhoades's, *Garden Crafts for Kids: 50 Great Reasons to Get Your Hands Dirty* (Sterling/Lark, 1995) to get ideas.

Grow peanuts in three different plots or buckets of soil in which the soil has been improved. For example, one plot could be regular garden soil to which nothing has been added; a second plot or bucket could contain soil that has been amended with commercial fertilizer; and a third plot or bucket could contain regular garden soil amended with your own compost. Raw peanuts can be purchased at an organic foods grocery store. Buckets of peanuts can be grown under plant lights. Discover under which conditions peanuts grow best.

Language Arts Activity

Plant Research

George Washington Carver developed 300 products from peanuts and 118 products from sweet potatoes. Plant scientists have developed many products from other plants such as soybeans. Research and create a chart that shows various plants and the products made from them.

Creative Activity

World's Fair Exhibit

In 1925, Alabama sent a peanut exhibit to the New York World's Fair. Use the information from your plant research chart to prepare an exhibit showing plants and their products for a hypothetical World's Fair. Use peanut butter play dough to create objects to include in your World's Fair exhibit.

Peanut Butter Play Dough
1 tablespoon honey
2 tablespoons confectioners' sugar
1 cup instant nonfat dry milk
1 cup creamy peanut butter
Mix until smooth. Refrigerate about 15 minutes until firm.

Treat

> # Homemade Peanut Butter
>
> Blend for 1 or 2 minutes in a blender or food processor:
> 1 cup shelled, roasted peanuts
> 1 1/2 Tbs. peanut oil
> 1/2 tsp. salt

Word Play

Arachibutyrophobia is the fear of getting peanut butter stuck to the roof of your mouth.

Read More About It

Coil, Suzanne M. *George Washington Carver.* Watts, 1990. 63 pp. (I).

Epstein, Sam, and Beryl Epstein. *George Washington Carver.* Garrard, 1960. 79 pp. (P-I).

McKissack, Patricia, and Frederick McKissack. *George Washington Carver: The Peanut Scientist.* Enslow, 1991. 32 pp. (P).

Rogers, Teresa. *George Washington Carver: Nature's Trailblazer.* Holt, 1992. 72 pp. (I).

Towne, Peter. *George Washington Carver.* Crowell, 1975. 33 pp. (P-I).

9.2 Johnny Appleseed

Lawlor, Laurie. *The Real Johnny Appleseed*. Whitman, 1995. 64 pp. (I). Illustrated by Mary Thompson.

Using government records and authentic historical research, Lawlor provides an accurate rather than a romanticized story of one of America's favorite characters, John Chapman—better known as Johnny Appleseed. Mary Thompson's woodcuts and engravings are augmented by engravings from the 1800s.

Gardening Activity

Sprout and Plant Apple Seeds

Say to your boys and girls, "It takes a long time for apple seeds to sprout. They will do so only if they have been chilled."

Allow a minimum of three months to complete this activity. Cut apples in half. Remove the seeds. Place the seeds in a covered container and refrigerate for about six weeks. After six weeks, place the seeds between two pieces of damp paper toweling and keep moist. When the seeds sprout, plant them about 1" deep in a pot filled with soil. Place in a sunny window. Water and fertilize the seedlings. Transplant them after they have sprouted true leaves. Be sure to place a collar around the young stem. A plastic yogurt cup with the end cut out will do.

Language Arts Activity

Tall Tales

People made up stories about Johnny Appleseed that grew into legendary tales after his death. Have your children make up their own tales about his bare feet, why he never married, and why he planted apple trees and helped people in the forest. Have them compare their tales with those written about Johnny Appleseed. Have them collect tall tales about other folk characters like Paul Bunyan, Pecos Bill, and John Henry.

Creative Activity

Choral Reading or Readers' Theater

Select passages from Meridel LeSueur's *Little Brother of the Wilderness* for choral reading or readers' theater.

Treat

Apple-Tasting Party

In her book *Better Known as Johnny Appleseed*, Mabel Leigh Hunt names nine varieties of apples that Johnny Appleseed may have planted: Fall Wine, Front Door, Nonesuch, Favorite, Northern Spy, Fallwater, Willow Twig, Sweet Bough, and Seek-No-Further. What varieties of apples are available where you live? Provide your boys and girls with a variety of local apples (or those grown in your state) to compare.

 ## Poem

Lindsay, Vachel. "In Praise of Johnny Appleseed." In *Johnny Appleseed and Other Poems*. Macmillan, 1967.

 ## Word Play

An epitaph is a phrase written on a person's tombstone or a brief statement commemorating that person. It often characterizes the person. Johnny Appleseed's epitaph states, "He lived for others."

Read More About It

Aliki. *The Story of Johnny Appleseed*. Prentice-Hall, 1963. 32 pp. (P).

Johnson, Ann Donegan. *The Value of Love*. Value Communications, 1979. 62 pp. (P-I).

Kellogg, Steven. *Johnny Appleseed*. Morrow, 1988. 42 pp. (P-I).

LeSueur, Meridel. *Little Brother of the Wilderness*. Knopf, 1958. 68 pp. (P).

Lindbergh, Reeve. *Johnny Appleseed*. Little, Brown, 1990. 32 pp. (I).

9.3 Beatrix Potter:
Author, Illustrator, Gardener

Taylor, Judy. *Letters to Children from Beatrix Potter.* Warne, 1992. 239 pp. (I).
This book is a charming and readable collection of letters written by Beatrix Potter to the many children in her life. It begins with letters written to the children of her former governess, which reveal the origins of her Peter Rabbit stories. These are followed by letters to her cousin's children, and finally by letters to children who wrote to her after reading her books. Photos, illustrations, and copies of letters supplement the transcriptions of Potter's letters. Explanatory statements tie the text together. Beatrix Potter's active interest in and warm affection for her readers can still draw today's children into her life and world.

 ## Gardening Activity

Observe and Record

Beatrix Potter was a student and observer of nature. Spend 15 minutes in your garden observing its life. Record what you see. Select one living thing to inspect closely. Draw a picture of it.

 ## Language Arts Activity

Letter Writing

Read *Letters to Children from Beatrix Potter* and engage in a conversation with Beatrix Potter by responding to her letters. Extend the activity by reading biographies about Potter. Pair boys and girls, with one taking the role of Beatrix Potter. Have them write letters to each other, one letter to Beatrix Potter, and the other from her. Encourage them to illustrate their letters with sketches and drawings as Beatrix Potter did.

 ## Creative Activity

Ballet

Have your boys and girls select or compose music and choreograph their own performance of a Peter Rabbit book of their own choosing. The ballet can be as simple or as elaborate as your group chooses. There are many opportunities to widen the activity to include set design, prop making, and costuming.

 ## Treat

Gingersnap Cookies

Serve gingersnap cookies. When Beatrix Potter's grandmother came to visit, she brought gingersnap cookies. They were Potter's favorite childhood treat.

Poem

Potter, Beatrix. "The Old Woman." In *A New Treasury of Children's Poetry,* ed. Joanna Cole. Doubleday, 1984.

Word Play

Beatrix Potter made up a secret code with which she wrote her journal for 12 years. Her secret code was finally cracked by Leslie Linder, who then edited and published her journals.

Read More About It

Aldis, Dorothy. *Nothing Is Impossible.* Atheneum, 1969. 156 pp. (I).

Buchan, Elizabeth. *Beatrix Potter.* Warne, 1987. 61 pp. (I).

Collins, David R. *The Country Artist.* Carolrhoda, 1989. 56 pp. (I).

Lane, Margaret. *The Tale of Beatrix Potter.* Warne, 1968. 173 pp. (I).

Linder, Leslie (Ed). *The Journal of Beatrix Potter: 1881-1893.* Warne, 1989. 468 pp. (I-Adult).

Potter, Beatrix. *Letters to Children.* Walker, 1966. 48 pp. (I).

9.4 Rachel Carson:
Biologist and Conservationist

Ransom, Candice F. *Listening to Crickets: A Story About Rachel Carson.* Carol-rhoda. 1993. 64 pp. (I).

This readable story about Rachel Carson tells of her love for nature and for writing. Born near Pittsburgh, Pennsylvania, she attended the Pennsylvania College for Women, where she studied literature and then biology. Fossils, marine life, ecology, and finally pesticides absorbed her interest. While her books about the sea brought her fame, it was her book *Silent Spring* that changed the public's view of the environment and resulted in the ban of DDT and other chemicals. Following her death in 1964, she was honored with a postage stamp issued in 1981.

Gardening Activity

Listen and Identify

Listen to and identify sounds of nature, such as birds, insects, wildlife, and wind.

Language Arts Activity

Discuss and Write

Jake Goldberg's *Rachel Carson: Biologist and Author* includes an excerpt from the fable with which she began *Silent Spring.* Present boys and girls with the question from that fable: "What would happen if you woke up to find that all birds and animals had died?" Encourage discussion, and then write a group response to the question.

Creative Activity

Music

Select or compose and perform music that represents the sounds of nature.

Treat

Trail Mix

Serve a trail mix of dried fruits and nuts. Boys and girls can enjoy this treat while listening to the sounds of nature.

Poem

Behn, Harry. "Crickets." In *Crickets and Bullfrogs and Whispers of Thunder,* ed. by Lee Bennett Hopkins. Harcourt, 1984.

Read More About It

Goldberg, Jake. *Rachel Carson: Biologist and Author.* Chelsea, 1992. 79 pp. (I).

Reef, Catherine. *Rachel Carson: The Wonder of Nature.* Holt, 1992. 68 pp. (I).

Ring, Elizabeth. *Rachel Carson: Caring for the Earth.* Millbrook, 1992. 48 pp. (I).

Wadsworth, Ginger. *Rachel Carson.* Lerner, 1992. 128 pp. (I).

Wheeler, Leslie A. *Pioneers in Change: Rachel Carson.* Silver Burdett, 1991. 137 pp. (I).

9.5 Other Plant and Nature Lovers

Lorbiecki, Marybeth. *Of Things Natural, Wild, and Free: A Story About Aldo Leopold.* Carolrhoda, 1993. 64 pp. (I).

Aldo Leopold acquired a love for nature from his father, who "read" stories from the land. Aldo became a bird-watcher and naturalist at an early age, graduated from Yale Forestry School in 1909, and began his career in the Apache National Forest of Arizona Territory. He developed conservation programs, became a wildlife scientist, and developed the Arboretum and the Department of Wildlife Management at the University of Wisconsin. He is the author of *A Sand County Almanac,* a collection of essays that express love for nature.

Gardening Activity

Visit an Arboretum

Visit an arboretum. Compile your own list of the different plants you find there.

Language Arts Activity

Research Careers

Research careers in forestry, conservation, plant science, biology, and botany. Ask the librarian or media generalist at your public or school library, or at your local arboretum, garden center, or botanical or zoological garden for assistance in collecting reference materials and developing your boys' and girls' basic reference skills.

Creative Activity

Collage

Make a collage of the different plants you find at the arboretum.

Treat

Nuts

Sample a variety of nuts, such as peanuts, walnuts, pecans, and almonds. How do they grow? Where do they come from?

Poem

Lindbergh, Reeve. *Johnny Appleseed.* Little, Brown, 1990. 32 pp.

Word Play

Many plants are named for people, often those who discovered them. Edward Palmer, botanist and collector, discovered 2,000 new plants. More than 200 species of plants, including the Palmer agave and the Palmer penstemon, were named in his honor.

Read More About It

Beaty, Janice. *Plants in His Pack: A Life of Edward Palmer, Adventurous Botanist and Collector.* Pantheon, 1964. 182 pp. (I).

Clarke, Brenda. *Children of History: Charles Darwin.* Cavendish, 1988. 31 pp. (P-I).

Meltzer, Milton. "People's Gardens: Frederick Law Olmstead and the First Public Parks." In *The Big Book for Our Planet,* ed. Ann Durell, Jean Craighead George, and Katherine Paterson. Dutton, 1993. 136 pp. (I).

Quackenbush, Robert. *Here a Plant, There a Plant, Everywhere a Plant, Plant! A Story of Luther Burbank.* Prentice-Hall, 1982. 35 pp. (P-I).

Rogers, Teresa. *George Washington Carver.* Holt, 1992. 72 pp. (I).

Bibliography

Annotations are provided for books mentioned in the "Read More About It" (RMA) sections. Annotations for books used in lessons (indicated by bold numbers) can be found in the lesson. Approximate grade levels are indicated in parentheses: P = Primary, K-3; P-I = Grades 2-4; I = Intermediate, Grades 4-6.

A

Aardema, Verna. *The Vingananee and the Tree Toad.* Warne, 1983. 48 pp. (P). RMA 8.4.

A tale from Liberia (where it was told by Aunt Clara, a beloved storyteller), it is the story of what happens when the Vingananee overcomes Rat, Buck Deer, and Lion. Tree Toad volunteers to take on the monster and by a miracle wins. Thus, domestic bliss is restored to Spider's house. This is a perfect story for telling with its sound effects and repeated phrases.

Abell, Elizabeth. *Flower Gardening.* Watts, 1969. 84 pp. (I). RMA 7.3.

A basic gardening book with information about rose culture not found in other books.

Aldis, Dorothy. *Nothing Is Impossible: The Story of Beatrix Potter.* Atheneum, 1969. 156 pp. (I). RMA 9.3.

The author brings to life Beatrix Potter, beginning with her lonely childhood and ending with her marriage to William Heelis. This biography is a readable and informative story that children will enjoy.

Aliki. *Corn Is Maize.* Harper, 1976. 34 pp. (P-I). RMA 6.5.

Corn, first grown by Central and South American people, is a versatile vegetable universally enjoyed. Aliki tells the story of corn's history, propagation, value, and uses. Her two-color illustrations echo corn's green and gold. At the end she gives directions for craft projects.

Aliki. *The Story of Johnny Appleseed.* Prentice-Hall, 1963. 32 pp. (P). RMA 9.2.

In this slightly romanticized tale, Aliki has emphasized Johnny Appleseed's peaceful nature as she tells of Chapman's trek across middle America in early pioneer days.

Aliki. *A Weed Is a Flower: The Life of George Washington Carver.* Prentice-Hall, 1965. 32 pp. (P). **9.1.**

B

Baptista, Lynn Hardie. *Discover Rain Forests.* Forest House, 1992. 44 pp. (P-I). RMA 5.4, 5.5.

This introduction to and overview of the rain forest, its habitats, and its plant and animal life will appeal to children of all ages. Five chapters focus on five topics, with informative text supplemented by full-color photos.

Beaty, Janice. *Plants in His Pack: A Life of Edward Palmer, Adventurous Botanist and Collector.* Pantheon, 1964. 182 pp. (I). RMA 9.5.

Born in England, Edward Palmer loved flowers more than anything else. When his brother decided that the family flowerbeds must be converted to a potato cash crop, Edward left for America, where flowers still grew wild. In New York, he met Dr. Jared Kirtland, who invited him to make his home in Cleveland, Ohio. From there Edward began a life of traveling and collecting plants. His travels took him to Paraguay, the southwestern United States, Mexico, Baja California, and finally to the Indian mounds of the eastern United States. By the time he died, he had collected more than 100,000 plants for the world's museums.

Bell, Corydon. *John Rattling Gourd of Big Cove.* Macmillan, 1955. 103 pp. (I). RMA 7.2.

Here's a book worth holding in every library possible because it preserves Cherokee tales that may not be found elsewhere. An old treasure trove, it contains the story of the origin of the Indian Peace Pipe (the plant) and the first strawberry.

Beskow, Elsa. *The Flowers' Festival.* Floris Books, 1991. 32 pp. (I). **8.3.**

Beskow, Elsa. *Peter in Blueberry Land.* Floris Books, 1987. unp. (I) RMA 8.3.

While looking for berries for his mother's birthday, Peter meets the King of Berryland and his sons, who take Peter berry picking in this whimsical fantasy.

Bjork, Christina, and Lena Anderson. *Linnea in Monet's Garden.* Raben and Sjorgren, 1978. 53 pp. (P-I). RMA 2.1, 2.3.

Linnea and Mr. Bloom visit Giverny. Mini-lessons in art, gardening, and Monet's life are provided by Linnea. The colorful photographs and illustrations heighten interest and information about using color in the garden.

Boden, Alice. *The Field of Buttercups.* Walck, 1974. 32 pp. (P). RMA 8.4.

In this picture book Boden retells an old Irish tale. Michael O'Grady has fallen for an old leprechaun's trick as he searches for a pot of gold in a field of buttercups.

Bordewich, Fergus M. *Peach Blossom Spring.* Green Tiger, 1994. 42 pp. (P-I). Illustrated by Yang-Yi. RMA 8.4.

Delicate paintings in Chinese style lure the reader into the book and down the river to a magical peaceful place found by a fisherman. The fisherman breaks his promise to the inhabitants when he tells others of this special place. When he returns, he cannot find it again.

Bown, Deni. *Orchids.* Steck-Vaughn, 1992. 47 pp. (I). RMA 2.2.

The varieties of, cultivation of, and geographic information about orchids are described in detailed text accompanied by attractive illustrations.

Brown, Deni. *Growing Herbs.* Dorling Kindersley, 1995. 80 pp. (I). RMA 3.3.

Describes the variety and cultivation of herbs.

Bradstreet, Brenda. *The Compact Herb Garden.* Solly's Choice, 1991. (P-I). RMA 3.3.

This small kit includes peat pellets and herb seeds, instructions for growing and using herbs, and a garden plan.

Briggs, Raymond. *Jim and the Beanstalk.* Coward-McCann, 1970. 40 pp. (P). RMA 8.5.

This is a contemporary sequel to the traditional tale, in which a young boy named Jim climbs the mysterious plant outside his bedroom window. Jim finds the toothless old giant in his castle complaining of his unhappiness since Jack stole his gold, his golden harp, and his golden hen. Jim helps the giant regain his happiness by obtaining false teeth, glasses, a wig, and new clothes for him. The giant rewards Jim with a gold coin and a thank-you note.

Brown, Marc. *Your First Garden Book.* Little, Brown, 1981. 48 pp. (P). RMA 4.2.

Jam-packed with ideas, this book will inspire children and the adults who garden with them to plant and create. Plant-related projects, especially ones that use recycled products, include milk-carton bird feeders, popsicle-stick labels, and old shoe planters. Gardening is not just for country kids; Brown has lots of ideas for city kids who want to plant. He gives a new-old definition to "crack" when he urges readers to plant Crack Gardens by sprinkling alyssum, portulaca, and morning glory seeds into the cracks of neighborhood sidewalks.

Bryan, Ashley. *Beat the Story-Drum, Pum-Pum.* Atheneum, 1980. 70 pp. (I). RMA 8.4.

The wisdom of African people is reflected in their stories, this time in a collection of folktales that Ashley Bryan has garnered from Nigeria. His striking woodcuts embellish the telling. Included is the story "Why Frog and Snake Never Play Together," which expresses the profound sadness caused by prejudice passed from parent to child.

Buchan, Elizabeth. *Beatrix Potter: The Story of the Creator of Peter Rabbit.* Warne, 1987. 61 pp. (I). RMA 9.3.

This biography of Beatrix Potter focuses on her love for the countryside, her animals, her studies, her stories, and her drawings. Photographs and illustrations supplement the text.

Buki, Ltd. *Our Garden.* Buki Toys, 1992. (P-I). RMA 2.5.

From a toymaker in Israel comes this plastic shape-maker and drawing book. It helps children discover and use plant shapes in arts and crafts projects.

Burke-Weiner, Kimberly. *The Maybe Garden.* Beyond Words, 1992. 21 pp. (P). Illustrated by Fredrika P. Spillman. **1.1.**

Burnett, Frances Hodgson. *The Land of the Blue Flower.* Kramer, 1993. 45 pp. (I). RMA 8.3.

The orphaned infant King Amor is raised by the Ancient One in a castle on the mountaintop. As he grows, Amor learns the stories of all things that grow. He learns to love the stars, the wind, and the animals. When he is crowned King, he discovers the meanness of his people and their lives. He decrees that all must plant and tend the seeds from a blue flower brought to him long ago by a sparrow from the walled garden. As the kingdom is transformed by the blue flower, so are the people.

Burnett, Frances Hodgson. *The Secret Garden.* Dell, 1990. 287 pp. (I). RMA 8.1.

Mary Lennox, a lonely child who comes to live in the cold household of Misselthwaite Manor, discovers a neglected garden. With the help of her physically disabled cousin, Colin, and her newfound friend, the wise Dickon, she brings the garden back to its old glory, while the family's emotional wounds are healed.

Burnie, David. *How Nature Works: 100 Ways Parents and Kids Can Share the Secrets of Nature.* Reader's Digest Association, 1991. 192 pp. (I). RMA 5.4.

A complete life science course for children ages 8 to 12, this book is packed with easy experiments and activities that will help children discover how plants, animals, and systems work.

C

Caduto, Michael, and Joseph Bruchac. *Native American Gardening.* Fulcrum, 1996. 158 pp. (I-Adult). **3.5.** RMA 6.5, 7.1.

Campbell, Mary Mason. *Kitchen Gardens.* Scribner's, 1971. 170 pp. (I-Adult). Illustrated by Tasha Tudor. RMA 1.3.

Tasha Tudor's charming illustrations embellish Campbell's essays and directions related to kitchen and herb gardens. Particularly delightful and applicable to garden design are her directions for designing a merry-go-round garden.

Carpenter, Frances. "The Golden Gourd." In *South American Wonder Tales.* Follett, 1969. pp. 64-70. (I). RMA 7.1.

This Brazilian folktale tells the story of two brothers: Silverio, who is very rich and mean-spirited, and Manoel, who is poor but honest. Manoel asks Silverio for land and is given a plot covered with thorns. On this land Manoel finds a golden gourd. He tells Silverio about it, but when Silverio goes looking for the gourd, all he finds is a wasp nest. Silverio tricks Manoel into locking himself in his hut. Silverio throws the wasp nest into the hut thinking that the wasps will sting Manoel to death. Instead the wasps turn into gold coins.

Carpenter, Frances. "The Poet and the Peony Princess." In *Tales of a Chinese Grandmother.* Tuttle, 1973. pp. 124-133. (I). **7.5.**

Carroll, Lewis. *Alice in Wonderland and Through the Looking Glass.* Messner, 1982. 253 pp. (I). RMA 8.3.

In this well-known and well-loved classic, Alice's fantasy-world adventures include meeting Tiger-lily, Rose, and Daisy in "The Garden of Live Flowers" and Gnat in "Looking Glass Insects." Their conversations lend themselves to acting out or to readers' theater.

Cathon, Laura E., and Thusnelda Schmidt. *Perhaps and Perchance: Tales of Nature.* Abingdon, 1962. 260 pp. (I). RMA 7.2, 7.5.

Cathon and Schmidt have compiled folktales, legends, myths, and poetry related to plants and animals. A treasure!

Center for Science in the Public Interest. Project Inside/Outside. *Ladybugs and Lettuce Leaves.* Center for the Study of Science in the Public Interest, 1982. 84 pp. (I). **3.4.**

Chase, Richard. "The Green Gourd." In *Grandfather Tales.* Houghton Mifflin, 1948. pp. 213-221. (I). RMA 7.1.

An old woman picks a green gourd that "witches" her. She runs to various forest animals calling upon them to save her. Finally, they all reach the bear's house; the bear sits on the gourd, which smashes it.

Chase, Richard. *The Jack Tales*. Houghton Mifflin, 1943. 201 pp. (I). RMA 8.5.

This classic collection of Jack tales includes the well-known variant, "Jack and the Bean Tree." Boys and girls will enjoy exploring the world of Jack.

Clarke, Brenda. *Children of History: Charles Darwin*. Cavendish, 1988. 31 pp. (P-I). RMA 9.5.

This biography of Charles Darwin begins with a short introduction and summary of Darwin's family, the influence of his grandfather, and Charles's controversial ideas of evolution. The book continues with the story of his life as a child, a collector, a schoolboy, a student voyager, and finally a scientist. The readable format includes margin notes, subheadings, illustrations, maps, index, and a timeline of important events in Darwin's life.

Cochrane, Jennifer. *Plant Ecology*. Bookwright Press, 1987. 47 pp. (I). RMA 5.1.

Eighteen topics including plants, photosynthesis, pollination, seed dispersal, plant succession, and habitats are addressed. The text continues with biomes, endangered plants, and pollution. A list of ecology related organizations is included. A good reference book.

Coil, Suzanne M. *George Washington Carver*. Watts, 1990. 63 pp. (I). RMA 9.1.

Just right for the intermediate grade reader, Coil's biography of Carver tells the story from his life-theatening childhood to how he overcame adversity in order to receive a university education. A love for learning, a strong sense of perseverance, and encouragement from freinds resulted in a successful career as a professor at Tuskegee Normal and Industrial School. There his research produced hundreds of uses for peanuts as well as the improvement of the sweet potato.

Cole, Joanna. *Plants in Winter*. Crowell, 1973. 32 pp. (P-I). Illustrated by Kazue Mizumura. RMA 7.4.

Cole explains why some trees lose their leaves in winter but why pine trees do not. She also shows what is going on underground and how bulbs, rhizomes, seeds, and roots stay protected until spring. Children come to know that winter plants are not dead.

Collins, David. R. *The Country Artist: A Story About Beatrix Potter*. Carolrhoda, 1989. 56 pp. (I). RMA 9.3.

This biography of Beatrix Potter tells the story of her lonely childhood, her love for the small animals who were her pets and companions, and of the journals and drawings that led to her books. The story of her adult years tells of her love for her farms and her marriage. The book concludes with a listing of her book titles.

Conaway, Judith. *City Crafts from Secret Cities*. Follett, 1978. 96 pp. (I). RMA 3.2.

A fascinating collection of craft projects based on archeological discoveries from archeologist and weaver Judith Conaway. For the purpose of garden-related activities, children may wish to try the "Courtyard Houses" or "A Dream Garden" activity.

Cooney, Barbara. *Miss Rumphius*. Viking, 1982. 32 pp. (P-I). RMA 8.2.

Miss Rumphius makes her world more beautiful by planting lupines wherever she can.

Courlander, Harold. *Uncle Bouqui of Haiti*. Morrow, 1942. 127 pp. (I). RMA 7.1.

A collection of humorous Haitian folktales featuring Uncle Bouqui, a town character and gardener who is always getting into a predicament. "Uncle Bouqui Goes Homesteading" tells the story of Uncle Bouqui's unhappiness with communal gardening.

Creasy, Rosalind. *Blue Potatoes, Orange Tomatoes*. Sierra Club Books, 1994. 40 pp. (P-I). Illustrated by Ruth Heller. **2.4.** RMA 2.3.

Crowell, Robert L. *The Lore and Legends of Flowers*. Putnam, 1982. 80 pp. (I). Illustrated by Anne Ophelia Dowden. RMA 7.2, 7.3, 7.5.

The stories of 10 beloved flowers are collected and retold. Dowden's illustrations distinguish this book as a collector's item. Included are tulips, narcissus, crocus, iris, carnations, roses, nasturtiums, dandelions, marigolds, and dahlias.

Cutler, Katherine. *The Beginning Gardener*. Barrow, 1961. 173 pp. (I). RMA 2.1.

Even though it is dated, Cutler's book has information that others do not, so it is worth your efforts to find it through interlibrary loan or urge librarians to bring it out from archival status. Particularly useful are the perennials and annuals lists in which these flowers are identified by color, thus helping the young landscape designer make decisions. For those interested in showing off, there is a chapter laying out the procedures for putting on an exhibition. Part 2 tells how to create specialty gardens. The plans for creating Bird, Box, Bulb, Dish, Friendship, Herb, Rock, Seashore, Terrarium, Wild Flower, and Window Gardens are described. For youngsters and their adult leaders searching for authentic ways to reach out to their communities, the chapter on setting up a Garden Information Center provides useful ideas.

Cutler, Katherine N. *Growing a Garden Indoors or Out*. Lothrop, Lee & Shepard, 1973. 96 pp. (I). RMA 1.4, 1.5.

Covers propagation, botany, and how to lay out and dig the garden plot. Includes lists of easy-to-grow plants and beneficial insects. Of particular note is Cutler's list of wildflowers in which she notes which ones not to gather. Of special value is chapter 5, in which Cutler invites children to share their plants with friends and neighbors through special gardens, gourd crafts, and potpourri, a value-centered attitude that is missing in many of today's gardening books.

D

Daddona, Mark. *Hoe, Hoe, Hoe. Watch My Garden Grow*. Addison-Wesley, 1980. 58 pp. (P). RMA 1.2, 4.2.

A basic how-to gardening book for boys and girls that covers how and where to site a garden, how to prepare the soil, and how to plant. Exclusively about vegetable gardening, it includes a section about starting vegetables from seeds indoors and transplanting. Last frost date information is given, which is not often found in other books.

D'Aulaire, Ingri, and Edgar P. Parin. *Book of Greek Myths.* Doubleday, 1962. pp. 58-63. (I). RMA 7.4.

The story of Demeter and Persephone is told and illustrated in the authors' distinctive, prize-winning style.

Davis, Brenda. *Newer and Better Organic Gardening.* Putnam, 1976. 95 pp. (I). RMA 5.2.

This book explains how to develop an organic garden with directions for composting, soil preparation, planting, and caring for crops. The appendix includes suggested books, seed sources, insect control, planting tables, and zone maps.

de la Mare, Walter. *The Turnip.* Godine, 1992. 32 pp. (I). Illustrated by Kevin Hawkes. **4.1.**

Demi. *The Empty Pot.* Holt, 1990. 32 pp. (P). RMA 7.5, 8.4.

Demi's delicate illustrations embellish her story of a young child's honesty. The emperor promises his throne to the child who can grow the most beautiful flowers from the seeds that he has provided. The children, eager for the prize, somehow grow beautiful flowers when in fact the emperor has boiled the seeds before distributing them to the children. Only one child, Ping, who has a reputation as a successful gardener, is not able to grow a beautiful flower. The emperor immediately recognizes him as honest. *The Empty Pot* is truly a book of virtue.

dePaola, Tomie. *Jamie O'Rourke and the Big Potato.* Putnam, 1992. 32 pp. (P). RMA 4.5.

In this Irish folktale we hear of lazy Jamie who won't dig up his potatoes, leaving this task to his wife. When she sprains her back and can work no more, Jamie believes he is faced with death by starvation, so he goes to the church. On his way he catches a leprechaun, who gives Jamie a potato seed for his freedom. Jamie plants the seed, which turns into the largest potato in the country. All the village has plenty to eat that winter.

dePaola, Tomie. *The Lady of Guadalupe.* Holiday House, 1980. 46 pp. (P-I). RMA 7.3.

As Juan Diego walked to the town of Tepeque for the church service, he saw a vision of Mary, Mother of God. The woman in the vision commands Juan Diego to convince the bishop to build a church in her honor. Juan Diego was not successful until the lady gave him a sign, Roses of Castile blooming at his feet. She bade him to pick the roses in his tilma, a cactus fiber cloth worn by the Aztecs and to take them to the bishop. When the bishop saw both the roses and the imprint of Our Lady Mary of Guadelupe on Juan Diego's tilma, he believed and had the church erected.

dePaola, Tomie. *The Legend of the Bluebonnet: An Old Tale of Texas.* Putnam, 1983. 32 pp. (P). RMA 7.2.

She-Who-Is-Alone sacrifices her only possession, a warrior doll with a blue feather, in order to end the drought and famine. As a sign that the drought has ended, the Great Spirit causes blue flowers to grow everywhere over the land we now know as Texas.

dePaola, Tomie. *The Legend of the Indian Paintbrush.* Putnam, 1988. 38 pp. (P). **7.2.**

dePaola, Tomie. *The Legend of the Poinsettia.* Putnam, 1994. 32 pp. (P). RMA 7.2.

When Lucida tangles the warp of the blanket her mother has been weaving as a gift to the church for the manger scene, she becomes distraught. Now her family has nothing to offer the Christ child. She gathers weeds growing outside the church. When she places the weeds around the manger, they turn into the red stars of the poinsettia blossom.

Dodge, Bertha. *Plants That Changed the World.* Little, Brown. 1959. 183 pp. (I). RMA 6.3.

The stories and history behind such plants as hemp, quinine, chocolate, and rubber are recounted. Using journal entries from explorers and botanists, Dodge presents historically accurate, highly detailed data. Readers learn of the medical and economic significance of the plants described. A worthwhile find despite its old publication date.

Donnelly, Liza. *Dinosaur Garden.* Scholastic, 1990. 32 pp. (P). RMA 3.4.

Dinosaur-loving Rex and his dog Bones plant a garden to attract dinosaurs. Their efforts pay off; not only do the dinosaurs appear, they even lay dinosaur eggs. Unfortunately, one of the eggs is that of a Tyrannosaurus mother who is not happy with Rex and Bones. They are rescued from this mad mother dinosaur by a Pterodactylus. All ends well. A glossary is included.

Doole, Louise Evans. *Herb Magic and Garden Craft.* Sterling, 1973. 192 pp. (I). RMA 1.3, 3.3.

The various shapes and designs that gardens can have are diagrammed and discussed. Geometric, ladder-shaped, and circular gardens are featured in this book about herb cultivation. With the older child in mind, Doole explains the varieties, cultivation, garden design, crafts, and recipes associated with herbs.

Dowden, Anne Ophelia. *This Noble Feast: A Chronicle of Herbs.* Collins, 1979. 80 pp. (I). RMA 3.3.

This history of mankind is entwined with the history of herbs. Dowden chronicles their importance to humans. More specficially, she relates their uses to physicians, housewives, and cooks down through the ages. Her beautiful watercolor paintings of many herb varieties will familiarize readers with their beauty.

Dowden, Anne Ophelia. *Poisons in Our Path: Plants That Harm and Heal.* HarperCollins, 1994. 61 pp. (I). RMA 6.1.

Plants both medicinal and poisonous are described and illustrated. The history and geographical origins of these plants are included.

Durell, Ann, Jean Craighead George, and Katherine Paterson (eds.). *The Big Book for Our Planet.* Dutton, 1993. 136 pp. (I). **5.1.**

E

Earle, Olive. *The Rose Family.* Morrow, 1970. 44 pp. (P-I). RMA 7.3.

The history, lore, and cultivation of the rose are explained along with strawberries, apple trees, and other members of this large plant family. Readers gain a broad notion about what's in a rose.

Ehlert, Lois. *Color Farm.* Lippincott, 1990. 32 pp. (P). RMA 1.3.

Ehlert uses diecut triangles, squares, rectangles, circles, and trapezoids to depict farm animals in this concept book.

Ehlert, Lois. *Growing Vegetable Soup.* Harcourt Brace Jovanovich, 1987. 32 pp. (P). RMA 4.4.

Visually exciting, this book gives the step-by-step process of growing 11 vegetables. A vegetable soup recipe is on the back cover.

Ehlert, Lois. *Planting a Rainbow.* Harcourt Brace Jovanovich, 1988. 24 pp. (P). **2.1.** RMA 2.3.

Elkington, John, Julia Hailes, Douglas Hill, and Joel Makowee. *Going Green: A Kid's Handbook to Saving the Planet.* Puffin, 1990. 112 pp. (I). RMA 5.1.

The authors have collaborated to produce this compilation of environmental issues, a checklist of environmental awareness, practical solutions, organizations, and a bibliography related to the environment.

Epstein, Sam and Beryl Epstein. *George Washington Carver.* Garrard, 1960. 79 pp. (P-I). RMA 9.1.

This warm, readable story of George Washington Carver tells how the sickly baby grew into a spindly child who tended the house and garden until the age of 13 when he set off to attend a nearby school. Driven by his desire to learn, he earned his way as he attended schools in Missouri, Kansas, and Iowa. He spent his career at Tuskegee Institute where he developed over 300 uses for peanuts.

Evans, David, and Claudette Williams. *Color and Light.* Dorling Kindersley, 1993. 29 pp. (P). RMA 2.3.

Simple experiments and demonstrations of the principles of color and light for the very young.

F

Facklam, Howard, and Margery Facklam. *Plants: Extinction or Survival?* Enslow, 1990. 96 pp. (I). RMA 6.4.

The importance of plants as a source of food, medicine, and other products is integrated with the research contributions made by both male and female scientists. Included is a chapter on medical technology.

Farmer, Penelope, and Graham McCallum. *The Story of Persephone.* Morrow, 1973. 48 pp. (I). RMA 7.4.
A retelling of the Persephone and Demeter myth.

Feeney, Stephanie. *Hawaii Is a Rainbow.* University of Hawaii Press, 1988. 60 pp. (P). Photographs by Jeff Reese. **2.2.**

Fell, Derek. *A Kid's First Book of Gardening.* Running Press, 1989. 96 pp. (I). RMA 1.4, 1.5, 2.4, 4.5.

Directions for planning and tending the garden as well as descriptions of varieties of odd colors and sizes of vegetables are provided. The author also gives information about trees and shrubs.

Fenten, D. X. *Gardening Naturally.* Watts, 1973. 87 pp. (I). RMA 5.2.

Organic gardening is treated in a serious, yet not too technical manner. Line drawings supplement and enrich this book written for the older and more serious young gardener. Topics include vegetable and flower garden cultivation, pest control, composting soil improvements, and garden cleanup.

Fenten, D. X. *Plants for Pots.* Lippincott, 1969. 128 pp. (I). RMA 1.4.

In addition to explaining different ways to propagate plants, Fenten describes the care needed for 12 house plants. He urges his readers to focus on a new plant each month.

Fenton, Carroll Lane, and Herminie B. Kitchen. *Plants We Live On.* John Day, 1971. 128 pp. (I). **6.1.** RMA 6.5.

Florian, Douglas. *Vegetable Garden.* Harcourt Brace Jovanovich, 1991. 32 pp. (P). RMA 4.1, 4.4.

This book, illustrated by the author, relates in a very easy-to-read rhyme the story of a family planting, caring for, and harvesting their vegetable garden.

Fryer, Lee, and Leigh Bradford. *A Child's Organic Garden.* Acropolis, 1989. 96 pp. (I). RMA 5.2.

Readers are encouraged to grow their own vegetables in a pesticide-free garden. Directions for improving soil are given. The text stresses environmentally safe practices.

Furlong, Monica. *Wise Child.* Knopf, 1987. 228 pp. (I). RMA 3.3.

A Scottish fantasy in which magic and witchcraft figure significantly, this is the story of Wise Child. Orphaned, she is sent by her village to live with Juniper, the villagers' magic woman. Juniper, a gardener and herbalist, teaches her skills and wisdom. The fantasy takes a dramatic turn when Wise Child's birth mother appears. The chapter titled "The Herb Garden" may be all you want to read aloud to boys and girls. Sophisticated youth who enjoy historical fantasy will appreciate this complex novel.

G

Galdone, Paul. *The Little Red Hen.* Houghton Mifflin, 1973. 44 pp. (P). RMA 8.1.

If you don't help out, you can't benefit from others' labor is the theme of this old folktale.

Gardiner, John R. *Top Secret.* Little, Brown, 1985. 110 pp. (I). RMA 8.2.

Allen Brewster does his science project on human photosynthesis, leading to quite an adventure. This is a wacky tale about a boy who turns himself into a plant. All the while Allen is dealing with the problems of turning green and sprouting roots, the Secret Service guys are watching him.

Garland, Sarah. *Peter Rabbit's Gardening Book.* Warne, 1983. 48 pp. (P-I) . RMA 3.1.

Explains the cultivation requirements of the plants mentioned in Beatrix Potter's stories. Used often as a guide by those who want to plant a Beatrix Potter or Peter Rabbit theme garden.

Garner, Alan. *Jack and the Beanstalk.* Doubleday, 1992. 32 pp. (P-I). Illustrated by Julek Heller. RMA 8.5.

British folkteller Alan Garner has rewritten this old tale, with its style, word choice, and rhythm reflecting the British perspective. Heller's vivid illustrations capture the personalities of the Big Woman, Jack, his mother, and the giant as well as the ancient setting.

Gary, Charles L., and Carol Watson. *Flower Fables.* EPM Publishers, 1978. 54 pp. (I). RMA 7.5.

This collection runs more to short folktales and legends, 28 in all, than to fables. Of particular interest is the morning glory and other time-related flowers for those gardeners who wish to plant a Telling Time Garden. Tales from Greece, China, and North America are included. Other flowers include yucca, corn, sunflowers, rose, peony, and dogwood. The story of the touch-me-not's ability to ward off poison ivy is told.

Gay, Kathlyn. *Cleaning Nature Naturally.* Walker, 1991. 137 pp. (I). RMA 5.2.

This readable book addresses topics such as working with nature, biological pest controls, and home pest management. It concludes with a list of organizations, suppliers of biocontrol products, a glossary, and an extensive biography.

Gentry, Linnea, and Karen Liptak. *The Glass Ark: The Story of Biosphere 2.* Viking, 1991. 94 pp. (I-Adult). **5.5.**

Giannini, Enzo. *Little Parsley.* Simon & Schuster, 1990. 32 pp. (P). RMA 3.3.

Little Parsley's mother steals parsley from the witches' garden, so they make her promise to give them her child. They give Little Parsley nearly impossible tasks to do. However, she is assisted by Cousin Nino, who always finds ways to succeed.

Gibbons Gail. *Nature's Green Umbrella.* Morrow, 1994. 32 pp. (P-I). RMA 2.2, 6.1.

World maps, carefully labelled illustrations, and readable text tell the story of the tropical rain forest. Corner illustrations depict familiar plants such as the orchid, hibiscus, bromeliads, and others native to the rain forest.

Gibbons, Gail. *Reasons for Seasons.* Holiday House, 1995. 32 pp. (P-I). RMA 7.4.

Gibbons provides a scientific explanation for seasonal changes as they deal with Earth's relationship to the sun. Her illustrations clearly show the critical angles and orbits. Connections to growth cycles are made.

Goldberg, Jake. *Rachel Carson: Biologist and Author.* Chelsea, 1992. 79 pp. (I). RMA 9.4.

Text and photos tell the story of Rachel Carson, pioneer founder of the ecology movement. Through her writings she inspired a public spirit of conservation. See page 53 for an excerpt from the fable with which she began *Silent Spring.* Present boys and girls with the question, "What would happen if you woke up to find that all birds and animals had died?"

Gove, Doris. *One Rainy Night.* Atheneum, 1994. unp. (I). Illustrated by Walter Lyon Krudop. RMA 5.4.

One rainy night in the mountains of North Carolina, a boy helps his mother, the director of a nature center, catch small animals for observation at the center. Toads, a newt, a water snake, grasshoppers, frogs, and salamanders come to life on the pages of this book, which delivers a message of environmental preservation and protection.

Graham, Ada, and Frank Graham. *Dooryard Garden.* Four Winds, 1974. 91 pp. (I). RMA 4.3.

Readers are taken through a gardening year with Tim and Jennifer. The text includes information about composting, planning, and laying out a garden, and a section about potato culture.

Grimm, William C. *Indian Harvests.* McGraw-Hill, 1973. 127 pp. (I). RMA 6.5.

Organized by plant families, the text is filled with details about the hundreds of plants gathered and used by Native Americans.

Guidetti, Geri. *A Seneca Garden.* KMG Publications, 1980. 24 pp. (I) RMA 3.5.

The history, lore, and design of a Three Sisters garden (corn, beans, and squash) are examined.

H

Halpern, Robert R. *Green Planet Rescue: Saving the Earth's Endangered Plants.* Watts, 1993. 64 pp. (I). **6.4.**

Handelsman, Judith F. *Gardens from Garbage.* Millbrook, 1993. 48 pp. (P-I). RMA 1.3.

For librarians, classroom teachers, and youth leaders who want to begin gardening with children but who do not want to go full-out with a 10'x12' summer-long garden, this may be just the book. Handelsman provides her readers with clearly described project after project that are simple and very affordable—she is talking about garbage after all—and guaranteed to be successful.

Harvey, Anne. *Shades of Green.* Greenwillow, 1991. 192 pp. (P-I). **2.5.**

Hays, Wilma, and R. Vernon Hays. *Foods the Indians Gave Us.* Ives Washburn, 1973. 113 pp. (I). **6.5.**

Henderson, Douglas. *Dinosaur Tree.* Bradbury, 1994. 32 pp. (P-I). RMA 3.4.

Text and illustrations explain the life cycle of a tree from the Triassic age and how it came to rest in the Petrified Forest of Arizona.

Hershey, Rebecca. *Ready, Set, Grow! A Kid's Guide to Gardening.* Goodyear, 1995. 104 pp. (P-I). RMA 1.2, 4.3.

Divided into three parts, this book tells children how to garden both indoors and outdoors. Acknowledging the current interest in connecting gardening with children's literature, Hershey includes a reading list with each of her activities. Craft activities and recipes are included in the third part.

Hirschi, Ron. *Saving Our Prairies and Grasslands.* Delacorte, 1994. 65 pp. (I). Photographs by Erwin and Peggy Bauer. RMA 5.3

The interdependence of habitat, animals, and humans is explained. Hirschi tells the story of specific endangered species. The growing habits of grasses and the relationship of certain grasses to specific animals are also described.

Hogner, Dorothy Childs. *Endangered Plants.* Crowell, 1977. 83 pp. (I). RMA 6.4.

Endangered plants are cataloged along with their descriptions and places where they can be found.

Holmes, Anita. *Cactus: The All-American Plant.* Four Winds, 1982. 192 pp. (I). RMA 6.1, 6.4.

The author shares her love for the desert and its many cacti by taking readers on a journey of discovery in this comprehensive resource. Graceful but detailed pencil drawings support the readable, informative text. Topics include adaptation to and role in the natural environment, distinguishing characteristics of various cacti as well as recipes and directions for raising.

Hughes, Monica. *A Handful of Seeds.* Lester, 1993. 32 pp. (P-I). Illustrated by Luis Garay. RMA 3.5.

After her grandmother dies, Concepcion leaves her country home for the city bringing seeds with her. Joining a band of other homeless children, she plants a garden. This first garden meets with disaster but soon Concepcion has a second garden planted and growing. She shares her harvest with other barrio children with the reminder to them to always save seeds for another planting.

Hunken, Jorie. *Botany for All Ages.* Globe Pequot, 1993. 184 pp. (I). RMA 5.4.

A complete botany course for the intermediate grades, the 9 to 13 year olds. The activites get the children out into their backyards, woods, meadows, parks, empty lots, and gardens to explore, observe, discover, ponder, ask questions, and communicate about nature. Plants, their parts, and functions are objects of discovery lessons. Respect for and understanding of the interdependence of plants, animals, habitat, and humans are stressed. This is an excellent manual for youth leaders, parents, and teachers searching for a complete, informative, and fun nature study program.

Hunt, Linda, Marianne Frase, and Doris Liebert. *Celebrate the Seasons.* Herald Press, 1983. 163 pp. (P-I). RMA 4.3.

Enchanting children's crayon drawings brighten an easy-to-follow text. Good gardening knowhow for children is organized around the seasons. The section on planning is helpful. The recipes will whet children's appetites for vegetables. Follow the little ladybug and gather a batch of helpful hints.

Hunter, C. W. *The Green Gourd: A North Carolina Folktale.* Putnam, 1992. 32 pp. (P). **7.1.**

I

Ichikawa, Satomi. *Nora's Roses.* Philomel, 1993. 32 pp. (P). RMA 7.3.

Nora, in bed with a cold, watches as many visitors come by her window to pick roses. She dreams that the rose fairies transport her to a fantasy party. At the story's end, Nora wishes for and finds a way to save one of the roses; she draws it. Reading this story aloud would be a fine way to introduce an art lesson.

Imagine a Biosphere: The Miniature World of Biosphere 2. Biosphere Press, 1990. (I). RMA 5.5.

Photos and graphics tell the story of this highly publicized experiment.

J

Jagendorf, M. A. "The Miracle of the Rose." In *The Priceless Cats and Other Italian Folktales.* Vanguard, 1956. 158 pp. (I). **2.3.**

Jernigan, Gisele. *Sonoran Seasons: A Year in the Desert.* Harbinger. 1994. unp. (P-I). RMA 5.6.

Using a two-page spread, full-page illustrations accompanied by a short verse for each month take the reader through a year in the Sonoran Desert.

Johnson, Hannah L. *From Seed to Salad.* Lothrop, Lee & Shepard, 1978. 48 pp. (I). **4.2.**

Johnson, Janice. *Rosamund.* Simon & Schuster, 1994. 32 pp. (P-I). Illustrated by Deborah Haeffle. **6.2.** RMA 7.3.

Johnson, Sylvia A. *Roses Red, Violets Blue: Why Flowers Have Color.* Lerner, 1991. 64 pp. (I). Photographs by Yuko Sato. **2.3.** RMA 2.4.

Johnson, Sylvia. *Wheat.* Lerner, 1990. 48 pp. (I). RMA 3.2.

Science writer Sylvia Johnson turns her attention to wheat, the most valuable food crop since ancient times.

Basic botany information about reproduction is enhanced by strobe-light and magnified photography.

Johnston, Tony. *The Tale of Rabbit and Coyote.* Putnam, 1994. unp. (P). Illustrated by Tomie dePaola. **8.4.**

K

Katz, Adrienne. *Naturewatch: Exploring Nature with Your Children.* Addison-Wesley, 1986. 128 pp. (I). RMA 2.5.

Written for both child and adult, this book tells the adult what to look for in meadow, seashore, woods, and garden and how to engage the child in observing and doing. In darker, larger print, directions for activities are provided: terrariums, botany experiments, windowboxes, gardening, sunflower cultivation, and plant crafts.

Kellogg, Steven. *Jack and the Beanstalk.* Morrow, 1991. 48 pp. (I). RMA 8.5.

Kellogg retells this old tale and illustrates it with colored ink, watercolor, and acrylic pictures.

Kellogg, Steven. *Johnny Appleseed.* Morrow, 1988. 42 pp. (P-I). RMA 9.2.

Vivid prose and lively pictures tell the story of John Chapman, who came to be known as Johnny Appleseed. A factual biography concludes with the retelling of legendary tales that sprang up about this well-loved personality.

Kite, L. Patricia. *Gardening Wizardry for Kids.* Barron's, 1995. 220 pp. (P-I). Illustrated by Yvette Santiago Banek. RMA 1.4, 2.5, 3.2, 3.3, 4.1, 4.3, 6.1, 6.2, 7.1, 7.2, 7.4.

This fun book is a boon for readers looking for authentic science experiments with plants. The book is divided into six parts: 1) "History and Folklore of Common Fruits and Vegetables"; 2) "Fun with Kitchen Fruits and Vegetables"; 3) "Indoor Plant Growing Experiments with Food Seeds"; 4) "Raising Earthworms, Pill Bugs, and Snails"; 5) "Herb History, Folklore, and Growing Instructions"; and 6) "Easy Plant Craft Projects."

Kohn, Bernice. *The Organic Living Book.* Viking, 1972. 72 pp. (I). Illustrated by Betty Fraser. RMA 5.2.

In this general approach to living without pesticides, watching what you eat, reading labels, and recycling are several chapters about organic gardening. The emphasis is on returning to the earth what has been removed and gardening without poisoning the soil, the plants, or the animal visitors.

Kramer, Jack. *Plant Sculptures.* Morrow, 1978. 63 pp. (I). RMA 2.5.

Kramer is up-front on the first page by stating that this activity may take two to six months and requires patience. He moves on to describe how to create animal shapes from 14-to 16-inch gauge wire that becomes the armature for plants such as *Ficus pumila, Hypocyrta strigilosa,* and *Columnea arguta.* An adult who wishes to do these projects with larger groups of children should enlist several other adult helpers. The thought of 30 undersupervised 11-year-olds whipping around 15-gauge wires gives one pause. Kramer wrote this book for individual youth seeking a new hobby.

Krauss, Ruth. *The Carrot Seed.* HarperCollins, 1945. 25 pp. (P). RMA 4.1.

Still a favorite among the pre-school and kindergarten set, this is the story of a young boy who plants a carrot seed and waits patiently for it to sprout.

Kroll, Steven. *The Biggest Pumpkin Ever.* Scholastic, 1984. 32 pp. (P). Illustrated by Jeni Bassett. RMA 4.5.

Clayton and Donald, mouse gardeners extraordinaire, take care of one pumpkin without the other knowing about it. Unfortunately, they have opposite goals: One wants a jack o' lantern; the other a prize at the fair. With help from their friend, they accomplish both.

Kuhn, Dwight. *More Than Just a Vegetable Garden.* Silver Burdett, 1990. 40 pp. (P-I). RMA 4.4, 5.3.

This photographic look at the changing world of the vegetable garden and the creatures that inhabit it includes simple instructions for starting a garden.

L

Lamb, Charles, and Mary Lamb. "Midsummer Night's Dream." In *Tales from Shakspeare.* Crowell, 1942. 360 pp. (I). RMA 8.3.

Charles and Mary Lamb retell the classic midsummer fantasy tale based on Shakespeare's play. Juice from the purple flower works magic when dropped on the eyelids. The magic potion causes a comedy of erroes among mismatched couples until the fairy king lifts the spell with a second potion.

Landau, Elaine. *Endangered Plants.* Watts, 1992. 60 pp. (I). RMA 6.4.

Landau draws her readers' attention to various endangered plants and recounts what efforts are being made to save them.

Lane, Margaret. *The Tale of Beatrix Potter: A Biography.* Warne, 1968. 173 pp. (I). RMA 9.3.

This biography of Beatrix Potter's life contains photos, watercolors, sketches, and reproductions of her letters. This book may be of greater interest to older children and young adults than to young children.

Lavine, Sigmund. *Wonders of Herbs.* Dodd, Mead, 1976. 64 pp. (I). RMA 3.3.

Lavine describes the cultivation and varieties of herbs. Also included is a section on herb fact and fiction. Did you know that you could pay your taxes with herbs? You could have, had you lived in the Holy Roman Empire when Charlemagne ruled.

Lawlor, Laurie. *The Real Johnny Appleseed.* Whitman, 1995. 64 pp. (I). Illustrated by Mary Thompson. **9.2.**

Leechman, Douglas. *Vegetable Dyes.* Webb, 1945. 55 pp. (I-Adult). RMA 3.5.

Drawing upon European and Native American knowledge of vegetable dying, the author has provided a manual for using North American plant material. Discussion of plant material, recipes for their use, and lists of dye plants and their colors are included.

Lerner, Carol. *A Biblical Garden.* Morrow, 1982. 48 pp. (I). RMA 3.2.

Botanical drawings depict 20 Old Testament plants still in existence. Botanical and Hebrew names, relevant Bible verses, and descriptive paragraphs are included.

LeSueur, Meridel. *Little Brother of the Wilderness.* Knopf, 1958. 68 pp. (P). RMA 9.2.

The author weaves facts and legends into tales of Johnny Appleseed authenticated by "my grandmother" who heard him singing, saw him pass, and even knew him. Boys and girls might enjoy selecting passages for choral reading or readers' theater.

Limburg, Peter. *What's in the Name of Flowers.* Coward, McCann & Geoghegan, 1974. 190 pp. (I). RMA 3.2, 6.1, 6.2.

From amaryllis to zinnia, stories about the names, histories, and growing habits of more than 50 flowers are described. The vignettes include information about the geographical origins of various flowers.

Lindbergh, Reeve. *Johnny Appleseed.* Little, Brown, 1990. 32 pp. (I). RMA 9.2.

A biographical poem and folk art convey the story of John Chapman (1774-1845), naturalist and missionary who distributed apple seeds from his nursery to settlers of the American frontier.

Linder, Leslie (ed.). *The Journal of Beatrix Potter: 1881-1893.* Warne, 1989. 468 pp. (I-Adult). RMA 9.3.

Leslie Linder cracked the code in which Beatrix Potter wrote her journals when she was 15 to 30 years old. Her journals reveal the hidden years of her life. This book will appeal to young adults.

Lorbiecki, Marybeth. *Of Things Natural, Wild, and Free: A Story About Aldo Leopold.* Carolrhoda, 1993. 64 pp. (I). **9.5.**

Lottridge, Celia Barker. *One Watermelon Seed.* Oxford University Press, 1986. 24 pp. (P). Illustrated by Karen Patku. RMA 4.2.

From Canada comes this delightful counting book based on a gardening theme. It takes the reader from 1 to 10 and then by tens to 100.

Lovejoy, Sharon. *Sunflower Houses.* Interweave, 1991. 144 pp. (I). **4.4.** RMA 1.3, 1.4, 2.1, 3.1, 4.2.

Lovejoy, Sharon. *Hollyhock Days.* Interweave, 1994. 95 pp. (I). **3.1;** RMA 1.1, 2.1, 7.1.

Lubell, Winifred, and Cecil Lubell. *Green Is for Growing.* Rand McNally, 1964. 64 pp. (P-I). RMA 2.5.

From algae to trees, green plants are named and described in rhythmic prose. Odd and unusual facts are dispersed throughout. Did you know that *Chicago* means "wild garlic," from the Winnebago Indians who called it shi-ka-ko?

Lucas, Jannette May. *Indian Harvest.* Lippincott, 1985. 118 pp. (I). RMA 3.5.

Full coverage of the wild plants gathered by woodland, prairie, and desert-dwelling Native Americans. It is worth the search you will need to locate a copy because it contains information about Native American horticultural practices that is rare to find in today's nonfiction for children.

M

Madgwick, Wendy. *Cacti and Other Succulents.* Steck-Vaughn, 1992. 47 pp. (I). RMA 1.4.

Madgwick describes the geographical origins and history of cacti and succulents. Growing habits, structure, and form are diagrammed.

Mamchur, Carolyn Marie, with Meguido Zola. *In the Garden.* Pemmican Publications, 1993. 48 pp. (P-I). Illustrated by Anne Hanley. RMA 3.5.

From Canadian authors comes this story of a fiesty native girl determined to make a garden. Despite setbacks and discouragement, Joyce, inspired by her grandmother's legacy, forget-me-not seeds, digs and hacks until she has a garden plot. The resulting produce is used to encourage her father's co-workers.

For parents and teachers looking for a cultural story to inspire perseverence and generosity, this story is a good choice.

Marshall, Virginia Stone. *Flower Arranging for Juniors.* Little, Brown, 1954. 113 pp. (I). RMA 3.1.

Clever connections to familiar folktales and songs make flower arranging for children easy and gamelike. Marshall introduces the four basic arrangement plans—the triangle, the crescent, the fan, and the reversed S curve—by recounting *Goldilocks and the Three Bears, Rock a Bye Baby, The Gingerbread Boy,* and *The Three Little Pigs.* She explains abstract concepts of design such as balance, color, and harmony so that young floral designers can easily relate to and understand them. Every decision in flower arrangement has a good reason behind it, which Marshall explains so that the designing process makes sense. Many suggestions specific to boys are scattered throughout.

McDermott, Gerald. *Daughter of Earth.* Delacorte, 1984. 32 pp. (P-I). RMA 7.4.

A retelling of the Demeter and Persephone myth in which a pomegranate makes all the difference.

McDonald, Lucille. *Garden Sass: The Story of Vegetables.* Nelson, 1971. 192 pp. (I). RMA 6.2.

McDonald presents well-researched vignettes about vegetables, their origins, uses, and lore. Although a few ideas seem dated to late twentieth century readers, this remains a treasure of the history, lore, and legends of 28 vegetables. It is fascinating reading to discover that tenth century Arabs cultivated carrots, that spinach was once a king's gift to a Chinese emperor, and that ancient Egyptians once built altars to worship the cabbage. Vegetables' importance to the world's health and wealth is recounted in McDonald's journalistic style. This book is a treasure of information not to be found elsewhere. It is readily available in the Pacific Northwest through inter-library loan.

McKissack, Patricia, and Frederick McKissack. *George Washington Carver: The Peanut Scientist.* Enslow, 1991. 32 pp. (P). RMA 9.1.

The McKissacks tell the story of Carver's accomplishments. The younger reader will enjoy the simply written text and gain information from the photographs.

McMillan, Bruce. *Growing Color.* Lothrop, Lee & Shepard, 1988. 40 pp. (P). RMA 2.3, 2.4.

Full-color photographs of vibrant fruits and vegetables teach young readers their color words.

Meltzer, Milton. *The Amazing Potato.* HarperCollins, 1992. 116 pp. (I). RMA 6.1.

Award-winning history writer Milton Meltzer focuses his talent on the potato, a lowly vegetable to which millions in the world owe their existence. Is that a grandiose claim? After reading this book about the potato's origin, history, cultivation requirements, and economic significance, boys and girls are likely to be impressed with this vegetable. Teachers, especially in intermediate-grade social studies, will appreciate the ease with which an integrated curriculum can be constructed around this theme.

Meltzer, Milton. "People's Gardens: Frederick Law Olmstead and the First Public Parks." In *The Big Book for Our Planet,* ed. Ann Durell, Jean Craighead George, and Katherine Paterson. Dutton, 1993. 136 pp. (I). RMA 9.5.

Thanks to the vision of William Cullen Bryant and Washington Irving, we now enjoy and perhaps take for granted the public parks in our cities and communities across the country. In 1856 the city of New York purchased a parcel of land and hired Frederick Law Olmstead to develop it into a park. Inspired by the public parks he had seen in Europe and the British Isles, Olmstead and his friend Calvert Vaux not only created Central Park but founded a new profession. Olmstead spent his life developing parks in major cities and preserving the natural settings of Niagara Falls, Yosemite, and the Adirondacks.

Millard, Adele. *Plants for Kids.* Sterling, 1975. 124 pp. (I). RMA 2.5.

Millard covers many topics and provides directions for a variety of projects. Vegetables in a windowbox, terrariums, bonsai, water gardens, as well as the usual sweet potato and avocado are included.

Milord, Susan. *The Kids' Nature Book: 365 Indoor/Outdoor Activities and Experiences.* Williamson, 1989. 158 pp. (I). RMA 2.1.

An activity for every day of the year. Susan Milord has compiled nature study, gardening, and craft activities that will keep the antsy 8-to-12-year old happy and occupied.

Mintz, Lorelie M. *Vegetables in Patches and Pots.* Farrar, Straus & Giroux, 1976. 116 pp. (I). RMA 5.2.

A comprehensive guide to organic vegetable gardening, the emphasis in this book is on natural pest control, good soil management, and timing. A guide to individual vegetable varieties and their care follows the how-to-garden section. Of particular value to city gardeners is the chapter on growing vegetables in odd containers. The 1970s was a high point for books about organic gardening for children, so persevere in your search for this one on public library shelves.

Mitchell, Andrew. *The Young Naturalist.* Usborne House, 1989. 32 pp. (I). RMA 1.2.

Information and activities for the young naturalist include experiments with plants, looking at flowers and trees, inviting animals to visit you, making and using collections, and nature through the camera's eye.

Morgan, Mary. *Benjamin's Bugs*. Bradbury, 1994. 44 pp. (P). **5.4.**

Murphy, Louise. *My Garden: A Journal for Gardening Around the Year*. Scribner's, 1980. 160 pp. (P-I). Illustrated by Lisa Campbell Ernst. RMA 7.5.
Gardening through the year with legends, poetry, and arts and crafts activities woven throughout. Lisa Campbell Ernst's woodcuts reinforce the idea that aesthetics and practicality are a winning combination.

N

Nash, Ogden. *The Animal Garden*. Evans, 1965. 44 pp. (I). RMA 1.1.
The humorist turns his attention to the garden and presents readers with a relative of Johnny Appleseed—only this gentleman enjoys creating fanciful gardens. Boys and girls will enjoy the word play, and it's sure to inspire even more word play activities.

Newton, James R. *A Forest Is Reborn*. Crowell, 1982. 28 pp. (P-I). RMA 5.1.
This book describes the reappearance of sun-loving plants and then trees as a Pacific Northwest forest is renewed after a fire.

Nichols Garden Nursery. *Profitable Gourd Crafting*. (I). RMA 7.1. (Available from Nichols Garden Nursery, 1190 South Pacific, Albany, OR 97321.)
Gives instructions on crafting and selling items made from gourds.

Norsgaard, E. Jaediker. *Nature's Great Balancing Act: In Our Own Backyard*. Cobblehill, 1990. 64 pp. (I). Photographs by Campbell Norsgaard. **5.3.**

Nottridge, Rhoda. *Sugar*. Carolrhoda, 1990. 32 pp. (P). RMA 6.2, 6.3.
Nottridge explains the importance of sugar in diet and health as well as traces the history of its cultivation. Sugar cane and sugar beet crops are depicted.

O

Ocone, Lynn, with Eve Pranis. *National Gardening Association Guide to Kids' Gardening*. Wiley, 1990. 148 pp. (I). RMA 1.2, 1.5.
One of the most authoritative books about children's gardening on today's market. It not only covers basic gardening but also makes connections to other curricular areas including science. This book is considered to be a bible for starting up school and community garden programs.

Oechsli, Helen and Kelly Oechsli. *In My Garden: A Child's Gardening Book*. Macmillan, 1985. 32 pp. (P-I). **1.2.**

Oppenheim, Joanne. *Floratorium*. Bantam, 1994. 48 pp. (P-I). Illustrated by S. D. Schindler. RMA 6.3.
Like a visit to a top-notch museum, this book takes the reader from one hall to the next as the various plant families, histories, and habitats are explored. Also included is a hall of fame that features the lives of botanical pioneers and important persons. This clever book inspires more lessons and activities.

P

Pallotta, Jerry. *The Flower Alphabet Book*. Charlesbridge, 1988. 32 pp. (P-I). Illustrated by Leslie Evans. RMA 7.5.
This is one of several science-related alphabet books by this author. Leslie Evans's gorgeous and brilliant illustrations and the detailed, fascinating notes about the lore of the flowers illustrated will appeal to young readers as well as adults.

Pallotta, Jerry. *The Spice Alphabet Book: Herbs, Spices and Other Natural Flavors*. Charlesbridge, 1994. 32 pp. (P-I). Illustrated by Leslie Evans. RMA 3.3.
Part of a series, this book is a treat to the eye as well as the taste-bud imagination thanks to Evans's illustrations.

Patent, Dorothy Hinshaw. *Flowers for Everyone*. Dutton, 1990. 64 pp. (I). Photographs by William Munoz. RMA 2.2.
Brilliantly colored photographs enliven a straightforward, factual text. Writing from the perspective of commercial flower growing, Patent describes how various commercially important flower varieties are propagated and marketed. Production of flowers on a large scale is emphasized. Teachers will find tie-ins to global education, economics, history, and geography as well as floriculture.
The orchid propagation and production section makes this book a valuable addition to a gardening book collection. Here the reader discovers two new ways of propagation: orchid seeds grown in a sugar gel and orchid plants reproduced by cloning.

Patent, Dorothy Hinshaw. *Yellowstone Fires: Flames and Rebirth*. Holiday House, 1990. 40 pp. (I). RMA 5.1.
Patent's photo-essay reports the fires of 1988, the aftermath, and the ecological future of the area.

Paterson, John, and Katherine Paterson. *Consider the Lilies*. Crowell, 1986. 96 pp. (I). Illustrated by Anne Ophelia Dowden. **3.2.**

Paul, Aileen. *Kids Outdoor Gardening*. Doubleday, 1978. 77 pp. (I). RMA 4.3.
Paul provides the necessary information for the youthful gardener to get started with a home-based hobby that is likely to last a lifetime. She talks about tools, compost, succession planting, and planting by the moon. Included are the directions for a play tent of chicken wire, posts, and gourd vines.

Pellowski, Anne. *Hidden Stories in Plants*. Macmillan, 1990. 93 pp. (I). RMA 2.2, 3.2, 4.1, 7.2.
A unique combination of folktales, myths, and legends with matching crafts enhances young people's observation and enjoyment of the botanical world. Simple diagrams accompany craft directions.

Porter, Wes. *The Garden Book*. Workman, 1989. 64 pp. (I). RMA 1.5, 4.4.
The book's designer knew that children would be dragging his little book (4 x 6") into the garden. It has a laminated cover to protect it. Full of practical suggestions, it tells how to create productive soil, how pollination works, how to plan a garden, how to transplant, and how to care for plants in the garden. Written for both the outdoor and indoor gardener, it contains a section on houseplants and terrariums.

Potter, Beatrix. *The Complete Tales of Beatrix Potter.* Warne, 1989. 383 pp. (P). **8.1.**

Potter, Beatrix. *Letters to Children.* Walker, 1966. 48 pp. (I). RMA 9.3.

Letters written by Beatrix Potter to her young friends Noel, Eric, and Freda Moore, the children of her former governess, reveal the origins of various stories and drawings that became the Peter Rabbit books. The book includes reproductions of nine handwritten letters and drawings with typescripts of the letters. The handwritten letters and drawings invite readers to step into the life and world of Beatrix Potter and to share her experience of becoming an author.

Potter, Beatrix. *Mr. Jeremy Fisher.* Warne, 1989. 59 pp. (P). RMA 8.1.

This is the classic tale of the frog who lives amidst the buttercups at the edge of the pond.

Potter, Beatrix. *The Tale of Peter Rabbit.* Penguin, 1989. 57 pp. (P). RMA 8.1.

This is the classic tale of Peter Rabbit who gets into Farmer MacGregor's garden.

Potter, Beatrix. *The Tale of Timmy Tiptoes.* Warne, 1989. 59 pp. (P). RMA 8.1.

Timmy Tiptoes is the little chipmunk suspected by the angry squirrels of having stolen their nuts.

Powell, E. Sandy. *A Chance to Grow.* Carolrhoda, 1992. 36 pp. (P-I). Illustrations by Zulma Davila. RMA 3.3.

A homeless family doesn't give up hope. Finally, they find a home, and the boy is able to find a spot for his garden box of herbs.

Priceman, Marjorie. *How to Make an Apple Pie and See the World.* Knopf, 1994. 32 pp. (P). RMA 6.1.

Children gain a lesson in geography and world agriculture as they find out how to make an apple pie in this whimsical picture book.

Pringle, Laurence. *Saving Our Wildlife.* Enslow, 1990. 64 pp. (I). RMA 5.3.

A look at efforts to protect wildlife and preserve habitats in North America emphasizes the relationship between animals and their environment.

Q

Quackenbush, Robert. *Here a Plant, There a Plant, Everywhere a Plant, Plant! A Story of Luther Burbank.* Prentice-Hall, 1982. 35 pp. (P-I). RMA 9.5.

Quackenbush tells the story of this pioneer of plant improvement.

Quattlebaum, Mary. *Jackson Jones and the Puddle of Thorns.* Delacorte, 1994. 113 pp. (I). RMA 8.2.

More than anything else, Jackson Jones wants a new basketball. His birthday is coming up and he can barely wait. His mother, who misses the country life of her childhood, wants her son to have the happiness she knew as a child when she had a garden. She gives Jackson Plot 5-1 at the Rooter's Community Garden. Not exactly a basketball! Jackson not only handles it well, he figures out a way to turn his plot into a business success but not before he dealing with major breaks and repairs with friends and one

enemy, Bood Green. Multicultural urban lifestyles are realistically and humorously portrayed.

R

Rahn, Joan Elma. *More Plants That Changed History.* Atheneum, 1985. 144 pp. (I). RMA 6.3.

Rahn traces the influence of paper, rubber, tea, tobacco, and opium on history.

Rahn, Joan Elma. *Plants That Changed History.* Atheneum, 1982. 144 pp. (I). **6.3.**

Ransom, Candice F. *Listening to Crickets: A Story About Rachel Carson.* Carolrhoda, 1993. 64 pp. (I). **9.4.**

Rapp, Joel. *Let's Get Growing.* Prince Paperbacks, 1993. 96 pp. (I). RMA 4.3, 7.3.

Rapp has written up 25 activities for children to try with both indoor and outdoor plants. Included are rose culture, cactus grafting, terrarium making, air layering, as well as basic gardening procedures.

Readman, Jo. *Muck and Magic.* Search Press, 1993. 48 pp. (P-I). Illustrations by Polly Pinder. **5.2.**

Reef, Catherine. *Rachel Carson: The Wonder of Nature.* Holt, 1992. 68 pp. (I). RMA 9.4.

Beginning with her campaign against the use of pesticides, this readable story about Rachel Carson emphasizes the interrelationship between living things and their environment.

Rhoades, Diane. *Garden Crafts for Kids: 50 Great Reasons to Get Your Hands Dirty.* Sterling/Lark, 1995. 144 pp. (I). **1.3.** RMA 4.4.

Ricciuti, Edward R. *Plants in Danger.* Harper & Row, 1979. 96 pp. (I). RMA 6.4.

This book begins with the story of a cactus seed that fell to the ground near the Spanish garrison town of Tucson, Arizona. The growth of the seed into a 200-year-old, 50-foot saquaro cactus parallels the growth of Tucson to a modern city. In this storylike manner using a historical perspective, the author examines both natural changes and destructive threats occurring to plant life in environments around the world and discusses the value of plant diversity.

Ring, Elizabeth. *Rachel Carson: Caring for the Earth.* Millbrook, 1992. 48 pp. (I). RMA 9.4.

"What if" questions launch this Rachel Carson biography. These lend themselves to lively speculation and discussion with boys and girls. It is a good read-aloud choice for younger boys and girls who may be interested in knowing that *The Tale of Peter Rabbit* was Rachel Carson's favorite book as a young child.

Rogers, Teresa. *George Washington Carver: Nature's Trailblazer.* Holt, 1992. 72 pp. (I). RMA 9.1, 9.5.

This biography of George Washington Carver begins with his journey from Ames, Iowa, to Tuskegee, Alabama, as he was about to begin his career as a teacher and plant scientist. He is portrayed as an environmentalist with a message of ecology—that all of nature is interrelated—and as a deeply religious man who saw himself as a trailblazer rather than a finisher. The book ends with lists of products that Carver developed from peanuts and sweet potatoes, a list of bulletins he published, a glossary, and an index.

Rylant, Cynthia. *This Year's Garden*. Aladdin, 1987. 32 pp. (P-I). RMA 7.4.

The annual gardening cycle is illustrated as family members plan their crops, plant the seeds, and watch their garden grow.

S

Sandburg, Carl. "How to Tell Corn Fairies When You See Them." In *Rootabaga Stories*. Harcourt Brace Jovanovich, 1988. pp. 169-76 (I). Illustrated by Michael Hague. RMA 8.2.

Vivid descriptions of corn fairies in their corn gold overalls by day, sewing new clothes by night with their big toes pointing to the moon, sitting between the corn rows, or running like the wind in the midst of a rain storm lend themselves to drawing, puppetry, or dramatic play.

Sawyer, Ruth. "The Legend of St. Elizabeth." In *The Way of the Storyteller*. Macmillan, 1968. pp. 307-315. (I). RMA 7.3.

Elizabeth distributes bread and wine to the needy. Her jealous mother-in-law, Sophie, tries to turn her son, Ludwig, against her. Ludwig forbids Elizabeth to distribute bread and wine to the hungry. One night he finds her in the garden; suspecting that she has bread and wine, he demanded to see what she has hidden in her mantle. There he finds white and red roses. Recognizing that a miracle has taken place, he begs her forgiveness.

Sedenko, Jerry. *The Butterfly Garden*. Villard, 1991. 144 pp. (I). RMA 3.1.

The author shares his love for butterflies and gardens in this informative resource book augmented by full-color photos. Topics addressed are the life cycle of butterflies, guides to butterflies, flowers, and plants with suggestions and designs for the butterfly garden. He includes appendices listing plants by mail, butterfly gardens to visit, butterfly organizations, native plant organizations, and suggestions for further reading.

Selsam, Millicent. *The Carrot and Other Root Vegetables*. Morrow, 1971. 48 pp. (P-I). RMA 4.1.

Life-cycle photographs and easy-to-read text depict the growth of carrots, turnips, beets, sweet potatoes, and other vegetables that grow underground.

Selsam, Millicent. *Cotton*. Morrow, 1983. 48 pp. (P-I). Photographs by Jerome Wexler. RMA 6.3.

Cotton, so absorbent and useful for clothing and cloth, is described and explained. Wexler's photographs provide even more insight. The history of the cotton gin and weaving is told, as are the cultivation and growth habits of cotton.

Selsam, Millicent. *Eat the Fruit. Plant the Seed*. Morrow, 1980. 48 pp. (P-I). Photographs by Jerome Wexler. RMA 3.2.

Shown through Jerome Wexler's photos are avocado, papaya, citrus fruits, mango, pomegranate, and kiwi fruit and their seeds. The planting and care of these fruits are described. Mail order sources are given so children can send away for them if they are not available locally. This is an excellent companion to *Cherries and Cherry Pits* by Williams and *Consider the Lilies* by John and Katherine Patterson.

Selsam, Millicent. *Peanut*. Morrow, 1969. 48 pp. (P-I). RMA 6.1.

The highly useful peanut has had a fascinating history, from its beginnings in Peru to a migration to Africa and then to the United States, where it became a very popular food. This book is a good choice to begin a thematic unit because Selsam makes the necessary connections to history, famous people, botany, geography, and economics.

Shanberg, Karen, and Stan Tekula. *Plantworks*. Adventure Publication, 1991. 159 pp. (I). RMA 5.4.

A wild plant cookbook, field guide, and activity book, this book is intended for the novice naturalist partnered with a parent or group leader. Plant identification, photographs, and craft and fun-with-words activities are included.

Siracusa, Catherine. *The Giant Zucchini*. Hyperion, 1993. 45 pp. (P). RMA 4.5.

Robert Squirrel and Edgar Mouse sing to a zucchini to encourage it to grow.

Siy, Alexandra. *Native Grasslands*. Dillon Press, 1991. 71 pp. (P-I). RMA 5.5.

This book takes a unique historical approach to the examination of the American grassland or prairie. It has several pages of suggested activities for continued inquiry. The names and addresses of environmental organizations are listed for more information about grasslands.

Slepian, Jan. *Risk 'n Roses*. Philomel, 1990. 175 pp. (I). **8.2.** RMA 7.3.

Sobol, Harriet. *A Book of Vegetables*. Dodd, Mead, 1984. 46 pp. (P-I). RMA 6.2.

Fourteen vegetables are described. The text conveys the history and uses of each vegetable. It would be appropriate to incorporate this book with a social studies lesson in which a world map is used to trace the geographical origins of each vegetable. The author and photographer intend that readers get beyond the grocery-store concept of vegetables.

Southgate, Vera. *The Little Red Hen*. Ladybird Books. 1987. 51 pp. (P). RMA 8.1.

Vera Southgate retells the story of the little red hen who finds and plants the wheat seed, raises and harvests the wheat, mills the flour, and bakes the bread all by herself. When her friends gather around to help her eat the bread after refusing to help with the work, she tells them that after working alone she will eat the bread alone.

Spier, Peter. *And So My Garden Grows*. Dell, 1969. 40 pp. (P-I). RMA 1.1.

Prize-winning illustrator Spier takes his readers on a tour of Italian gardens. The locations are identified in the notes at the end of the book. A study of these illustrations will give boys and girls a different view of garden designs. Mother Goose rhymes comprise the text.

Sterling, Dorothy. *The Story of Mosses, Ferns, and Mushrooms*. Doubleday, 1955. 159 pp. (I). RMA 3.4.

What do mosses, ferns, and mushrooms have in common? They are flowerless. They represent some of the oldest plant lifeforms on the earth today. In Sterling's book, readers will find the history of plant life as well as photographs of ferns, mosses, and mushrooms found in today's woods and forests. This is a book for the serious young botanist who is seeking lots of detailed information.

Stevens, Janet. *Top & Bottoms*. Harcourt Brace, 1995. 34 pp. (P). RMA 8.4.

An old African folktale about a lazy bear and a bevy of trickster rabbits has been retold and drolly illustrated by Stevens. This amusing tale, with its lively, humorous pictures, is guaranteed to captivate young gardening readers. A perfect tale for storytellers.

Stevenson, James. *Grandpa's Too-Good Garden*. Greenwillow, 1989. 32 pp. (P). **4.5.** RMA 1.1.

Still, James. *Jack and the Wonder Beans*. Putnam, 1977. (P-I). RMA 8.5.

This is an Appalachian Jack tale.

Stone, Doris. *A Kid's Guide to Good Gardening*. Brooklyn Botanic Garden, n.d. 45 pp. (P-I). RMA 1.5.

This pamphlet for young gardeners is part of a kit produced by the Brooklyn Botanic Garden for their gardening program. The kit contains a videocassette and another booklet titled *Ideas for Parent's and Teachers*. For more information write to Brooklyn Botanic Garden, 1000 Washington Avenue, Brooklyn, NY 11225, or call them at (718) 622-4433.

Stone, Lynn M. *Wetlands*. Rourke Enterprises, 1989. 48 pp. (I). RMA 5.5

This is an informative introduction to wetland ecosystems such as marshes, swamps, and bogs. It includes types and locations of wetlands, plant and animal life, a discussion of how the ecosystem came to be, and conservation.

Sunset Editors. *Sunset Best Kids Garden Book*. Sunset, 1992. 96 pp. (P-I) **1.4.** RMA 1.2.

Sutcliff, Rosemary. *Chess-Dream in a Garden*. Candlewick, 1993. 48 pp. (I). Illustrated by Ralph Thompson. RMA 1.1.

In this fantasy legend the forces of evil enter the peaceful garden. The white king and his knights fight back valiantly and win.

Swenson, Allan. *Big Fun to Grow Book*. McKay, 1977. 170 pp. (I). **1.5.**

T

Taylor, Judy. *Letters to Children from Beatrix Potter*. Warne, 1992. 239 pp. (I). **9.3.**

Thomas, Elizabeth. *Green Beans*. Carolrhoda, 1992. (P). RMA 8.2.

Grandma's green beans refuse to grow until she goes on vacation. Children will enjoy having this story read to them. Grandma is one for the rules but she forgets a big one for gardeners. Sometimes you just have to let nature take its course.

Tilgner, Linda. *Let's Grow!* Storey Communications, 1988. 208 pp. (I). RMA 1.3, 1.4, 4.2.

Here are 72 garden activities for children. Native American gardening, making cornhusk dolls and scarecrows, planting a fruit tree, growing mold gardens, making sunprints, and pressing flowers are just a few of the many lively activities included. Sound gardening advice and instructions are given. The photographs of highly enthusiastic

young gardeners motivate readers to try their hand at the projects. Especially worth noting are the suggestions for working with very young children and children with disabilities.

Towne, Peter. *George Washington Carver*. Crowell, 1975. 33 pp. (P-I). RMA 9.1.

George Washington Carver became know as the "Wizard of Tuskegee" for his many contributions as a plant scientist. Upon arrival at Tuskegee Institute, he built a laboratory from scraps retrieved from the school's junk pile, taught his students to enrich the soil, developed tasty food from the cowpea, built a wagon school with which he visited farmers' homes, encouraged farmers to plant peanuts, and developed nearly 300 useful peanut products.

Tolstoy, Alexei. *The Great Big Enormous Turnip*. Watts, 1968. 34 pp. (P). Illustrated by Helen Oxenbury. RMA 4.1.

Oxenbury's droll illustrations brighten this ancient Russian cumulative tale of a family who try to pull up a great big turnip. Lots of repetitive lines make this an ideal story for beginning readers. A writing activity using the sentences would make a natural follow-up.

Turner, Ann. *Grasshopper Summer*. Macmillan, 1989. 176 pp. (I). RMA 8.2.

In this story narrated by 11-year-old Sam, the reader learns of life in the Dakota Territory of 1874. Building a sod house and planting crops are described in detail.

V

Van Allsburg, Chris. *The Garden of Abdul Gasazi*. Houghton Mifflin, 1979. 33 pp. (P-I) RMA 8.3.

Alan's dog ran away into the fantasy-like garden of a magician. Did the story really happen or is this Alan's fantasy?

Van Allsburg, Chris. *Just a Dream*. Houghton Mifflin, 1990. 48 pp. (P-I). RMA 5.1.

Walter, who is clueless and indifferent about caring for the environment, is transformed by a dream. He wakes up literally and figuratively and changes his habits.

Verey, Rosemary. *The Herb Growing Book*. Little, Brown, 1980. 41 pp. (I). **3.3.**

Vogelgesang, Jennifer. *Discovering Deserts*. Forest House, 1992. 44 pp. (P-I). RMA 5.5.

This introduction to an overview of the desert, its life, and its resources will appeal to children of all ages. Each page focuses on a specific topic with informative text augmented by full-color photos.

W

Wadsworth, Ginger. *Rachel Carson*. Lerner, 1992. 128 pp. (I). RMA 9.4.

Wadworth's biography of Rachel Carson portrays her love of nature, the simplicity and power of her writing, and the clarity of her research, which first angered the public and then the chemical industry. Later it helped to shape federal legislation designed to protect the environment.

Waldherr, Kris. *Persephone and the Pomegranate*. Dial, 1993. 32 pp. (P-I). **7.4**

Walking Night Bear and Stan Padilla. *Song of the Seven Herbs*. Book Publishing Company, 1987. 60 pp. (I). RMA 3.5.
The Native American legends associated with stinging nettle, yarrow, dandelion, violet, chicory, wild rose, and sunflower are recounted here.

Walsh, Anne B. *A Gardening Book: Indoors and Outdoors*. Atheneum, 1976. 100 pp. (I). RMA 1.3.
Described in this book are a variety of gardens: kitchen, herb, and salad basket. Of particular value are several recipes for various soils: cactus soil, terrarium soil, and potting soil. Also included are designs and plans for a variety of gardens such as kitchen and herb.

Walters, Jennie. *Gardening with Peter Rabbit*. Warne, 1992. 46 pp. (P-I). **4.3.**

Waters, Marjorie. *The Victory Garden Kids' Book*. Globe Pequot, 1994. 148 pp. (I). RMA 1.2.
A comprehensive book about gardening for and about children, the text conveys information about site selection, soil testing, soil preparation, planting, weeding, harvesting, and preparing the garden plot for winter. Side bars tell of crops for different climates, buying seedlings, and window box gardening. The book includes excellent sections about composting, measuring rain, beneficial insects, and how to grow the biggest pumpkin. The second half of the book describes individual vegetables and flowers from basil to zucchini. A special feature of this book is The Yardstick Garden. In every chapter Waters provides information about constructing and caring for a 3-foot by 3-foot garden that is planned step-by-step for beginning gardeners.

Westcott, Nadine B. *The Giant Vegetable Garden*. Atlantic Monthly, 1981. 32 pp. (P). RMA 4.5.
In a gardener's fantasy, the villagers allow their vegetables to grow so profusely that the village is threatened.

Wexler, Jerome. *From Spore to Spore: Ferns and How They Grow*. Dodd, Mead. 1985. 48 pp. (P-I). RMA 2.5, 3.4.
Wexler's text conveys information about the fern's life cycle and gives advice on cultivating them.

Wheeler, Leslie A. *Pioneers in Change: Rachel Carson*. Silver Burdett, 1991. 137 pp. (I). RMA 9.4.
Wheeler tells the story of Rachel Carson, who became a marine zoologist and inspired the ban against poisonous pesticides. Her crusade to preserve the balance of nature shaped public awareness of the environment. This book is likely to appeal to older boys and girls.

Wiesner, David. *June 29, 1999*. Clarion, 1992. 32 pp. (P-I). RMA 1.1.
Holly Evans attaches her vegetable seeds to balloons that will take them to the ionosphere. On June 29, giant vegetables fall from the sky. Was this part of her experiment?

Wilbur, C. Keith. *Indian Handcrafts*. Globe Pequot, 1990. 144 pp. (I). RMA 3.1, 3.5, 6.5.
Among descriptions of handicrafts are directions for gourd cultivation and craft.

Wildsmith, Brian and Rebecca Wildsmith. *Jack and the Meanstalk*. Knopf, 1994. unp. (P-I). **8.5.**

Wilkes, Angela. *My First Green Book*. Random House, 1991. 48 pp. (P). RMA 5.3.
Wilkes presents activities and experiments about the importance of green plants to Earth's oxygen supply. She describes how to create a wildlife garden.

Wilson, Charles M. *Green Treasures: Adventures in the Discovery of Edible Plants*. Macrae Smith, 1974. 184 pp. (I). RMA 6.3.
Here is a fascinating account of the people who put food on our table. It is a compilation of the stories of agricultural pioneers who discovered and/or improved edible plants that could be developed for commercial production.

Wilson, Gilbert. *Buffalo Bird Woman's Garden*. Minnesota Historical Society, 1987. 129 pp. (I-Adult). RMA 3.5.
Originally published in 1917, this is an oral history of Hidatsa Indian agricultural practices and related activities as told to anthropologist Gilbert Wilson by Buffalo Bird Woman. The Hidatsa Indians were Plains Indians who raised corn, squash, beans, sunflowers, tobacco, potatoes, and other vegetables along the Missouri River bottomlands of North Dakota. Planting, growing, harvesting, storing, and preparing foods are described. Customs, rituals, stories, songs, and ceremonies are introduced in this readable account of a Native American gardening year's activities.

Wittstock, Laura Waterman. *Ininatag's Gift of Sugar: Traditional Native Sugarmaking*. Lerner, 1993. 48 pp. (I). RMA 3.5.
The Anishinabe people have a legend that tells hows Ininatag, the man tree, spoke to a starving family and told them how to make maple syrup. In photographs and text, a step-by-step explanation is given of a family's life in a Minnesota sugar bush. Readers see how a tree is tapped, the sap gathered, and the syrup created.

Wolf, Janet. *The Rosy Fat Magenta Radish*. Little, Brown, 1990. 32 pp. (P). RMA 4.1.
Nora, with the help of her neighbor, Jim, plants a vegetable garden. She alone plants a special row of radish seeds that take a long time to sprout. The endpapers display garden tools, an idea group leaders may wish to incorporate in book-creating projects.

Wyler, Rose. *Science Fun with Peanuts and Popcorn*. Messner, 1986. 48 pp. (P-I). RMA 6.5.
Experiments with peanuts and popcorn enable boys and girls to learn how plants grow. Information is included about the origins and history of peanuts and popcorn and the work of George Washington Carver. The book concludes with suggestions for a party with games, recipes for refreshments, and tongue twisters.

Y

Yolen, Jane. *Welcome to the Green House*. Putnam, 1993. 32 pp. (P-I). Illustrated by Laura Regan. RMA 5.3.
Regan's lush, emerald-green illustrations portray the flora and fauna of the tropical rain forest. Yolen explains the interconnectedness of the rain forest creatures and their environment.

Activities Index

Creative Activity

Gardening Activity

Author/Title/Subject Index

Listed here are those books and authors mentioned in the text as well as general subjects. Numbers in bold refer to lesson number. The "Bibliography" contains a full listing of authors and books used for the lessons and "Read More About It" sections.

About the Authors

Nancy Allen Jurenka

Nancy Allen Jurenka is co-founder of G.A.R.D.N., Gardeners and Readers Develop Naturally, a Special Interest Group of the International Reading Association. She teaches children's literature and reading education courses at Central Washington University in Ellensburg, Washington, where she is Professor of Education. Previously, she taught at Chapman University in Orange, California. She is a past-president of California Professors of Reading.

Her undergraduate degree is from Wilson College in Chambersburg, Pennsylvania. She received her master's degree from Western Connecticut University, and her doctorate from Indiana University. She has taught in Connecticut, Nevada, California, Indiana, Ohio, and Washington. ˙

Nancy is a Master Gardener and has worked with the children's gardening program at the arboretum in Yakima, Washington. She is the co-author with Rosanne Blass of *Responding to Literature: Activities for Grades 6, 7, and 8* (Englewood, CO: Teacher Ideas Press, 1991) and *Beyond the Bean Seed: Gardening Activities for Grades K-6* (Englewood, CO: Teacher Ideas Press, 1996).

Rosanne Johnson Blass

Rosanne Blass is a Visiting Professor in the College of Education at the University of South Florida, St. Petersburg. Dr. Blass completed her master's and doctoral degrees at the University of Tennessee after receiving her bachelor's degree at the University of Minnesota. Her experience includes teaching in public, private, and parochial schools in Minnesota, Michigan, Tennessee, Pennsylvania, Ohio, California, Arizona, and Florida. She is the co-author with Nancy Jurenka of *Responding to Literature: Activities for Grades 6, 7, 8* (Englewood, CO: Teacher Ideas Press, 1991) and *Beyond the Bean Seed: Gardening Activies for Grades K-6* (Englewood, CO: Teacher Ideas Press, 1996).

143

from Teacher Ideas Press

BEYOND THE BEAN SEED: Gardening Activities for Grades K–6
Nancy Allen Jurenka and Rosanne J. Blass

Engaging book-based lessons integrate gardening, children's literature, and language arts through creative activities embellished with poetry, word play, and recipes. The projects lead to learning in a variety of other subjects—from ecology, history, and geography to career exploration and the sciences. Also includes an annotated bibliography of resources related to gardening. **Grades K–6**.

xiv, 195p. 8½x11 paper ISBN 1-56308-346-9

EXPLORATIONS IN BACKYARD BIOLOGY: Drawing on Nature in the Classroom, Grades 4–6
R. Gary Raham

Young learners will discover life science adventures in their own backyards (or school yards) with this new resource! After reading brief descriptions of fascinating creatures, students participate in hands-on explorations with exciting classroom and field activities. Using drawing and writing skills, they record their experiences in a Naturalist's Notebook, which facilitates further discoveries. A fun and user-friendly approach to science. **Grades 4–6**.

xix, 204p. 8½x11 paper ISBN 1-56308-254-3

SCIENCE THROUGH CHILDREN'S LITERATURE: An Integrated Approach
Carol M. Butzow and John W. Butzow

Highly recommended.—**The Book Report**

The best book I have come across for the integration of science and literature.—**Science and Children**

Instructional units integrate all areas of the curriculum and serve as models to educators at all levels. Adopted as a supplementary resource in schools of education nationwide, this best-seller features more than 30 outstanding children's fiction books that are rich in scientific concepts yet equally well known for their strong story lines and universal appeal. **Grades K–3**.

xviii, 234p. 8½x11 paper ISBN 0-87287-667-5

GLUES, BREWS, AND GOOS: Recipes and Formulas for Almost Any Classroom Project
Diana F. Marks

Offers hundreds of practical, easy and classroom-tested recipes that can be used in a variety of curricular areas.—**Arts & Activities**

Pulling together hundreds of practical, easy recipes and formulas for classroom projects—from paints and salt map mixtures to volcanic action concoctions—these kid-tested projects make learning authentic and enjoyable. All projects use ingredients that are easy to find and processes that are up-to-date. Tips on when, why, and how to use these terrific concoctions are also included. **Grades K–6**.

xvi, 179p. 8½x11 paper ISBN 1-56308-362-0

ART PROJECTS MADE EASY: Recipes for Fun
Linda J. Arons

Tools to whip up some fun.—**Curriculum Review**

Fun, quick, and easy as pie, these art lessons provide an entire year of art activities! Using a variety of media, students explore art principles, collage, crafts, drawing, painting, holiday and seasonal art, multicultural art, and curriculum connections. **Grades 1–6**.

xv, 165p. paper ISBN 1-56308-342-6

STORYCASES: Book Surprises to Take Home
Richard Tabor and Suzanne Ryan

Combining books with manipulatives and activity ideas, the authors put it all together in such containers as bags, boxes, and cookie tins so students can learn at home with family members. Step-by-step instructions guide educators in assembling these simple kits called storycases. **Grades K–2**.

xix, 161p. 8½x11 paper ISBN 1-56308-199-7

For a free catalog or to order these or any other TIP titles, please contact:
Teacher Ideas Press • Dept. B16 • P.O. Box 6633 • Englewood, CO 80155-6633
Phone: 1-800-237-6124, ext. 1 • Fax: 1-303-220-8843 • E-mail: lu-books@lu.com

More Activity Books